Study Guide

for

Spatz's

Basic Statistics
Tales of Distributions
Eighth Edition

Chris Hakala
Western New England College

Chris Spatz
Hendrix College

THOMSON
—————— ™
WADSWORTH

Australia • Canada • Mexico • Singapore • Spain • United Kingdom • United States

Printer: Darby Printing

0-534-61138-9

Cover image: Phil Schermeister/CORBIS

For more information about our products,
contact us at:
Thomson Learning Academic Resource Center
1-800-423-0563

For permission to use material from this text or product,
submit a request online at
http://www.thomsonrights.com.
Any additional questions about permissions can be
submitted by email to **thomsonrights@thomson.com.**

Thomson Wadsworth
10 Davis Drive
Belmont, CA 94002-3098
USA

Asia
Thomson Learning
5 Shenton Way #01-01
UIC Building
Singapore 068808

Australia/New Zealand
Thomson Learning
102 Dodds Street
Southbank, Victoria 3006
Australia

Canada
Nelson
1120 Birchmount Road
Toronto, Ontario M1K 5G4
Canada

Europe/Middle East/South Africa
Thomson Learning
High Holborn House
50/51 Bedford Row
London WC1R 4LR
United Kingdom

Latin America
Thomson Learning
Seneca, 53
Colonia Polanco
11560 Mexico D.F.
Mexico

Spain/Portugal
Paraninfo
Calle/Magallanes, 25
28015 Madrid, Spain

For the women in his life, Chris Hakala dedicates this book to
Tammy Hakala
Abigail Hakala
Lillian Hakala

With love and affection, Chris Spatz dedicates this book to
Mark Christopher Spatz
Kenneth Siria Spatz
Elizabeth Ann Spatz

I would like to thank many people who contributed to my ability to complete this study guide. My wife and children were patient and supportive throughout the entire process. Kayla Convery, my student assistant, helped with the logistics and with some typing. My colleagues at WNEC were very helpful, especially Kathy Dillon who introduced me to Chris Spatz and proofread parts of the study guide. I would also like to thank Chris Spatz for allowing me to work with him on this project. Finally, I would like to thank the Duda brothers for helping me put the finishing touches on this book.

Chris Hakala
May 31, 2004

It is a pleasure to acknowledge the help I've received on this study guide. Hendrix College students worked problems and found errors. Nicole Loggans assisted on this book, the textbook, and the Student CD. Dwight Sigsbee volunteered his help. Dr. Thea Spatz contributed ideas and encouragement. Some work of Dr. James O. Johnston, my co-author in early editions, remains. I received valuable support from Hendrix College colleagues.

Chris Spatz
May 31, 2004

Contents

Preface

This study guide accompanies the eight edition of the textbook, *Basic Statistics: Tales of Distributions*, by Chris Spatz. The purpose of this study guide is to provide you with review, explanations, and problems to work. For most people, practice and repetition are required before they reach that plateau where they can say, "I understand; let me explain it to you."

Each chapter begins with a one-to-three page summary of the major points in the corresponding chapter of the textbook. Key words are in italics. Additional explanations are provided for the concepts that students have trouble with. The problems that follow the summary are divided into three groups: (1) multiple-choice questions (about 20 per chapter); (2) short answer or interpretation questions; and (3) problems that require calculation as well as interpretation.

The multiple-choice questions emphasize concepts. Some of them are not easy. The short-answer questions range from simple listing to paragraph explanations. Interpretation questions describe data or a simple experiment and then ask for an explanation. The problems are designed to provide practice on several things: choosing the right statistical test, applying formulas and doing the arithmetic, and interpreting the analysis using the terms of the problem.

Many of these problems are modeled after published research such as classical studies or recent, interesting reports. The answers to the odd-numbered problems are in the back of the study guide. The answers to the even-numbered problems are in the Instructors Manual and Test Bank.

This new edition of the study guide reflects the efforts of the senior author, Chris Hakala of Western New England College. All chapters have additional multiple-choice questions. Many short answer interpretation questions are new and additional problems were added to selected chapters. All the problems in Chapter 15, which gives students practice in choosing statistical tests, are new.

Acknowledgments are always in order when a book is published. Together, we acknowledge Jennifer Wilkinson and her staff at Wadsworth who did their usual good job of converting a manuscript into an attractive book. We also have a separate list of people to acknowledge.

If you find errors in this study guide, please report them to us at spatz@hendrix.edu. We will post corrections at http://www.hendrix.edu/statistics8thED.

CHAPTER 1

Introduction

Summary _____

The overall purpose of the first chapter of the textbook is to introduce

    1. broad categories and important terms used in statistics (for example, descriptive and inferential statistics, parameter, independent variable),

    2. the organization of the book.

In addition to the usual introductory definitions, the text discussed the place that statistics occupies in various disciplines that utilize statistics. We hope that by seeing the number of areas that use statistics, we will convince you of the value of this course. The kind of reasoning that people use when they do statistics problems may be applied to many other situations that aren't the least bit statistical. Because of the general applicability of statistics, you will benefit if you use your best efforts in this course.

    Statistics is a dynamic discipline. There are changes in the practice of statistics (such as changing from hand calculators to computers), and in theoretical applications (such as the notion of how to interpret different statistical tests). One of the goals of the text is to provide you with a snapshot of statistics in the early 21st century and help you understand how statistics have evolved into their current state. No doubt statistics will continue to change in the future!

    The notion of *descriptive statistics* is pretty simple and straight-forward: a single number is used to capture a particular characteristic of a set of data. *Inferential statistics* is a set of procedures that allow you to make a decision about a population even though all your information comes from a sample. The assumption with inferential statistics is that your results are influenced by change and random factors that are not under your control. With inferential statistics, you can make predictions that are likely to be true, but cannot be proved absolutely.

Chapter 1

The idea of using a *sample* as a substitute for a larger, unmeasurable *population* will be found in every chapter that follows. The characteristics of samples, *statistics*, and the characteristics of populations, *parameters*, are easy to keep straight. The two *p's* go together and the two *s's* go together.

Quantitative and *qualitative variables* find their way into the text in several chapters after this first one. Quantitative variables have *lower* and *upper limits* and are expressed in amounts. Qualitative variables have names and are expressed as kinds. The names in a qualitative variable may or may not have the characteristic of order.

With a *ratio* scale of measurement, a zero means a complete absence of the thing measured. Also, ratio statements such as "twice as much" and "reduced by one-third" make sense. Such ratio statements don't make sense if the variable is measured on an *interval* scale. Also, for interval scales, zero is just a convenient starting place; it doesn't mean zero amount. Like the ratio scale, however, equal distances on interval scales represent equal amounts of the variable.

For variables measured with *ordinal* scales, equal distances between numbers do not mean equal amounts of the variable. A larger number means more, but it doesn't tell you how much more. The difference between 5 and 10 on an ordinal scale is not the same as the difference between 10 and 15. *Nominal* scales have the least information of all. On a nominal scale, different numbers mean only that the things being measured are different.

If you understand the topic of *experimental design*, you can plan the procedures necessary to gather data. If you understand the topic of *statistics*, you can analyze the data. A good researcher should be able to do both well.

The distinctions between *independent, dependent*, and *extraneous* variables, which are troublesome for many students, will appear again and again, both in the text and in your academic career. Do all the study guide problems that ask you to make these distinctions.

Epistemology is the study of knowledge. Some knowledge is created by using reason, one example of which is a technique called statistics.

Chapter 1

The text's abbreviated 200-year history of statistics concentrates on the beginnings of institutions and the beginnings of statistics courses. Can you cite some dates? Four levels of competence in statistics are described. Can you list them? As described earlier, statistics is a dynamic discipline. It will continue to change and develop.

You will probably spend several hours with this study guide. Your study guide notes will be valuable during the course, as you prepare for any final examinations, and in future courses that use statistics. If you have any comments or suggestions, please e-mail Chris Hakala at chakala@wnec.edu.

Multiple-Choice Questions_____

1. Inferential statistics allow a researcher to
   (1) select representative samples;
   (2) make decisions about populations;
   (3) characterize a set of data with one number or name;
   (4) all of the above.

2. The Zeigarnik effect
   (1) is the distinction between statistics and experimental design;
   (2) is that numbers mean different things depending on the scale of measurement;
   (3) is a phenomenon of memory;
   (4) all of the above.

3. Which of the following was not described as a benefit of a course in statistics?
   (1) conclusions may be made with certainty;
   (2) a tool used in several disciplines is learned;
   (3) you get an education in decision making;
   (4) you are better able to communicate with others.

4. _____ are used as estimates of parameters
    - (1) Statistics;
    - (2) Constants;
    - (3) Populations;
    - (4) Upper limits.

5. Five means more than three on the
    - (1) ordinal scale;
    - (2) interval scale;
    - (3) ratio scale;
    - (4) all of the above.

6. Many schools rank their graduates each year from highest to lowest. Graduates wind up with scores such as 21 and 111. Such a scale is one example of a(n) _____ scale.
    - (1) nominal;
    - (2) ordinal;
    - (3) interval;
    - (4) ratio.

7. On the _____ scale, zero means a complete absence of the thing measured.
    - (1) ordinal;
    - (2) interval;
    - (3) ratio;
    - (4) all of the above.

8. Epistemology deals with the nature of
    - (1) reason;
    - (2) experience;
    - (3) mathematics;
    - (4) knowledge.

Chapter 1

9. In a study of the effect of handedness on athletic ability, participants were divided into three groups: right-handed, left-handed, and ambidextrous. Athletic ability was measured on a 12-point scale. The independent variable is_____; the number of levels of the independent variable is
   (1) athletic ability; three;
   (2) athletic ability; twelve;
   (3) handedness; three;
   (4) handedness; twelve.

10. In the study of handedness and athletic ability, the dependent variable is
    (1) handedness;
    (2) athletic ability;
    (3) not described;
    (4) both (1) and (2).

11. When numbers are used as substitutes for names, the numbers constitute a(n) _____ variable.
    (1) qualitative;
    (2) quantitative;
    (3) extraneous;
    (4) independent.

12. If an experiment has two groups of participants and if both groups are "chronic schizophrenics," then chronic schizophrenia is most likely a(n)
    (1) independent variable;
    (2) dependent variable;
    (3) controlled extraneous variable;
    (4) any of the above are likely.

13. In an experiment to determine the effect of a stimulant on amount of time spent studying, an extraneous variable would be
    (1) the stimulant;
    (2) the time spent studying;
    (3) both (1) and (2);
    (4) neither (1) nor (2).

Chapter 1

14. A statistics student is interested in determining if studying in the room where class is held improves scores on a statistics exam. To do this, she has half the class study in their normal seats and the other half study in their rooms. In this experiment, an example of an extraneous variable would be
    (1) room temperature;
    (2) where the students studied;
    (3) both (1) and (2);
    (4) neither (1) nor (2).

15. In an experiment on the effect of sleep on memory, the independent variable might be
    (1) number of hours of sleep;
    (2) recall score on a test;
    (3) gender of the subjects;
    (4) gender of the experimenter.

16. Which of the following were listed among Kirk's four levels of statisticians?
    (1) computer programmers who specialize in statistics;
    (2) psychologists who apply statistical techniques;
    (3) mathematical statisticians who develop statistical techniques;
    (4) all of the above.

17. According to your text, the reason for doing an experiment using samples is to
    (1) find out about the sample;
    (2) find out about the population;
    (3) obtain numbers so that statistics may be calculated;
    (4) obtain numbers so that parameters may be calculated.

Chapter 1

18. A researcher is interested in understanding differences between men and women on attitudes towards employment after the age of 70. To do this study, the experimenter asks 50 adults aged 25-30 to respond to a series of open ended questions. The experimenter then takes the data and looks for themes that correspond to her theory of personality. The variables measured in this study are
    (1) quantitative variables;
    (2) basic variables;
    (3) applied variables;
    (4) qualitative variables.

19. What level of measurement would I use if I were to ask every member of my class what state they were born in, then count up the number from each state?
    (1) Nominal;
    (2) Ordinal;
    (3) Ratio;
    (4) Interval.

20. Which of the following is a description of an independent variable?
    (1) number of rat's tail flicks;
    (2) amount of aggression demonstrated by a participant following a video;
    (3) whether or not a student takes a drug or a placebo;
    (4) all are independent variables.

Short-Answer Questions _____

1. Distinguish between
   a. descriptive and inferential statistics;
   b. populations and samples;
   c. interval and ordinal scales of measurement.

2. What is the difference between qualitative and quantitative variables?

Chapter 1

Problems _____

1. Undergraduates conducted each of the following studies. Identify:
   a. the independent variable
   b. the number of levels of the independent variable and their names
   c. the dependent variable
   d. a controlled extraneous variable
   e. a variable measured with a nominal scale
   f. another variable and the scale used to measure it
   g. Write an explanation of what the study shows.

   A. Natalie covered the walls of three small rooms with red, blue, or white paper. Participants in her study entered a room, worked on 3 difficult logic problems for 10 minutes, and then filled out a mood survey. For the 36 participants, the mood survey scores ranged from 10 (calm) to 40 (agitated). The mean mood scores for the three rooms were red-24; blue-16; white-18.

   B. Khiela interviewed 60 students who were about her age (20). She used a questionnaire that allowed her to classify the parenting style of the parents of those she interviewed. The parenting style classifications were authoritarian, authoritative, and permissive. After filling out the questionnaire, the students indicated their grade point average (GPA). An inferential statistical test did not reveal any statistically significant differences among the three groups.

2. Undergraduates conducted each of the following studies. Identify:
   a. the independent variable
   b. the number of levels of the independent variable and their names
   c. the dependent variable
   d. a controlled extraneous variable
   e. a variable measured with an ordinal scale
   f. another variable and the scale used to measure it
   g. Write an explanation of what the study shows.

Chapter 1

A. Social loafing occurs when people don't work as hard in a group as they work alone. For example, three people pulling on a rope exert less force than the sum of the three pulling individually. Kaycee wondered if social loafing occurs when the task is cognitive rather than physical. All participants worked at small tables in groups of three. Each individual worked on a word square (a 15 x 15 array of letters) for six minutes searching for 20 words hidden in the word square. Half of the 30 participants were told that the words they found would be averaged with the other two people at their table; the other half were told that their words were scored individually. The number of words circled was recorded for each participant; the mean was 7.6 words for participants working in groups and 9.6 words for participants working alone.

B. Blaine was interested in the relationship between food spiciness and personality characteristics. The participants in Blaine's study were women who had not eaten for at least 3 hours. They first tasted three dips (with chips). One was mild, another medium, and one was hot. After indicating a preference, the participants filled out a risk survey that indicated their desire to engage in activities such as skydiving, bungee jumping, and driving fast. The three groups averaged about the same score on the risk survey.

3. What are the lower and upper limits of the following numbers?
   a. 1.3 minutes
   b. 8 errors
   c. 23°F
   d. $45.50
   e. 10.00 grams

4. The following pairs represent the lower and upper limits of what numbers?
   a. 4.5-5.5
   b. 6.35-6.45

Chapter 1

c. .815-.825
d. 0.5-1.5
e. 652.35-652.45

5. Identify the kind of scale that each set of values comes from.
    a. Lieutenant, Captain, Major
    b. anxiety disorder, phobic disorder, adjustment disorder
    c. 50, 100, 250
    d. 0°C, 20°C, 40°C
    e. hat, shirt, shoes, pants
    f. 1st place, 2nd place, 3rd place
    g. 5 meters, 10 meters, 150 meters

6. Identify the scale of measurement for the items that follow.
    a. achievement-test scores
    b. numbers assigned to identify groups in an experiment
    c. numbers given to different sections of the same course
    d. win, place, and show in a horse race
    e. dollar amounts in a bank statement
    f. rank order of teams in a sport based on wins and losses
    g. amount of liquid in a fluid ounce

7. Identify each measurement below as being based on a quantitative or qualitative variable. For quantitative variables identify the lower and upper limits of the measurement.
    a. 414, dollars received from a part-time job
    b. 16, cubic yards of dirt
    c. 8, identification for Druid College among private schools in Transylvania
    d. 3.0, millions of dollars in the budget
    e. 101.9, km/hr registered on a radar machine used by the state police
    f. 23.95, the time in seconds required for Sam to swim 50 yards
    g. 4 minutes, 15 seconds, time to run a mile
    h. 0.87, percentage of material recalled from a text

8. Identify the quantitative variables below by writing in lower and upper limits on their blank lines. Write qualitative beside the variables that deserve such a name.
   a. 2 styles of sonnets   _____
   b. 3 feet of paper   _____
   c. 4 species of protozoa   _____
   d. 5.0 seconds of time   _____
   e. 6.05 grains of gold   _____
   f. 7.95 decibels of noise   _____
   g. 100 points on an IQ test   _____
   h. 118 wins in a season by a baseball team   _____
   i. 24 ways to describe love   _____

9. A classic experiment by Warden (1931) measured the motivation of rats for food, water, or sex. After deprivation, a rat had to cross an electrified grid to get to the goal object. (The whole apparatus was called the Columbia Obstruction Box.) The amount of electrical shock a rat would tolerate and still cross was measured. (Thirst came out as the strongest motive.) Name the dependent and independent variable. Identify an extraneous variable that should have been controlled.

10. The importance of early psychic traumas of children as a precursor of cancer has been investigated. Psychic traumas were those in which emotional relationships brought pain and desertion. Of 450 cancer patients, 72% had experienced such an early psychic trauma. Only 10% of a non-cancerous control group reported such an experience. Name the independent variable and dependent variables and at least one extraneous variable that should have been controlled.

CHAPTER 2

Frequency Distributions and Graphs

Summary _____

When you understand the material in this chapter, you will be able to:
1. organize a set of measurements into a frequency distribution
2. construct an appropriate graph
3. identify graphs by name and recognize the direction of skew, if any

This chapter starts by describing a set of unorganized scores and proceeds with methods of organization techniques of descriptive statistics. The unorganized Personal Control scores were compiled into a *simple frequency distribution* table, which was then further compiled into a *grouped frequency distribution* table. Constructing class intervals for grouped frequency distributions is explained in Appendix B in the textbook.

Graphs are a different (and sometimes superior) way to present frequency distributions and other relationships among variables. Frequency distributions give information about one variable and can be presented as a frequency polygon, a histogram, or a bar graph. *Frequency polygons*, which show data points connected by lines, and *histograms*, which have bars raised to the appropriate frequency, are both used for *quantitative* data. Bar graphs, which have separated bars raised to the appropriate frequency, are used for *qualitative* data. A *line graph* is used to present the relationship between two variables.

Several graphs were described with words and figures. The names for *bell-shaped* curves and *J-curves* are descriptive. *Skewed distributions* are unbalanced in one direction, *bimodal distributions* have two humps, and *rectangular distributions* are flat on top.

Remember the caution in the textbook. Drawing a graph requires effort. Draw a graph with a variety of scales and then choose one that conveys the information best. A poorly designed graph gives a false impression of the scores, but a properly constructed graph allows the reader to see the relationship between variables.

Chapter 2

Multiple-Choice Questions_____

1. The graph that is used to present data on two variables rather than one is the
   - (1) frequency polygon;
   - (2) histogram;
   - (3) bar graph;
   - (4) line graph.

2. Assume you give a survey to college students examining attitudes towards dress codes in high schools. Students rate their attitudes on a scale of 1-5. When the data are initially collected, the raw scores could be organized into
   - (1) a grouped frequency distribution;
   - (2) a simple frequency distribution;
   - (3) a *j* curve;
   - (4) both (1) and (2).

3. The best way to determine if a graph is a histogram or a bar graph is to look at
   - (1) the height of the bars;
   - (2) whether the bars are wide or narrow;
   - (3) the kind of variable on the Y axis;
   - (4) the kind of variable on the X axis.

4. To present a frequency distribution of nominal data you should use
   - (1) a frequency polygon;
   - (2) a bar graph;
   - (3) a histogram;
   - (4) a line graph.

5. Which of the following is *not* used to present a frequency distribution?
   - (1) bar graph;
   - (2) histogram;
   - (3) frequency polygon;
   - (4) line graph.

Chapter 2

6. In psychology, we sometimes measure parenting style. There tends to be general agreement that there are three main types of parenting style: Authoritarian, authoritative, and permissive. If we surveyed every person at the college and determined parenting style, we could put these data in a frequency distribution. This is a frequency distribution of a(n) _____ variable.
   - (1) nominal;
   - (2) ordinal;
   - (3) interval;
   - (4) ratio.

7. A distribution with two separated peaks is a _____ distribution; one that is severely skewed is a _____ distribution.
   - (1) J curve; rectangular;
   - (2) rectangular; bimodal;
   - (3) bimodal; J curve;
   - (4) J curve; bell-shaped.

8. The fact that the middle of a series of items is more difficult to learn than the beginning or the end is known as the
   - (1) series effect;
   - (2) middling effect;
   - (3) bimodal effect;
   - (4) serial position effect.

9. Suppose a frequency distribution with a range of 0 to 100 was positively skewed. The greatest frequency of scores would be expected around
   - (1) 25;
   - (2) 50;
   - (3) 75;
   - (4) any of the above are possible for such a distribution.

10. Skewness refers to
   - (1) the shape of the curve;
   - (2) the number of items in the curve;
   - (3) the standard error of the curve;
   - (4) none of the above.

Chapter 2

11. When a curve has a shape with two peaks, it is called
    (1) normal;
    (2) skewed;
    (3) rectangular;
    (4) bimodal.

12. The horizontal axis of a graph for a frequency distribution is called
    (1) a line graph;
    (2) the ordinate;
    (3) the abscissa;
    (4) a histogram.

13. Assume you collect data from psychology majors who indicate their favorite class in psychology. Students choose from five classes. What kind of graph should you use to display the data?
    (1) histogram;
    (2) bar graph;
    (3) line graph;
    (4) not enough information to answer this question.

14. Grouped frequency distributions and simple frequency distributions differ in
    (1) the type of data displayed;
    (2) the range of scores covered by the distribution;
    (3) the conclusions that can be drawn about skewness;
    (4) all of the above.

15. Graphs are popular because they
    (1) allow comparisons to other studies when designing a project;
    (2) help guide future research;
    (3) serve as a clear description of previous research;
    (4) all of the above.

Short-Answer Questions _____

1. In four sentences, distinguish among the frequency polygon, the histogram, the line graph, and the bar graph.

Chapter 2

2. For each situation, decide which of the four types of graphs is most appropriate. After your answer, write your reason.
   a. a telephone poll of 100 houses to determine what TV show the person is watching;
   b. a telephone poll of 100 houses to determine household income;
   c. average number of hospital admissions for each day of the week in New York City;
   d. numbers reported by each member of a large sociology class when asked, "How many close friends do you have?"
   e. number of correct answers on a psychology exam;
   f. income level of people who score high on an IQ test.
   g. attendance figures at a political debate, a ballet, a dramatic production, and a rock concert, all of which were held on the same night;
   h. number of calories you consumed over a four-week period;
   i. number of people entering a museum each hour it is open;
   j. number of people entering each of four pizza restaurants during one hour.

Problems _____

1. For each distribution of scores, 1) compile a simple frequency distribution, and 2) identify the shape of the distribution or the direction of skew.
   A. 9, 10, 9, 9, 11, 9, 10, 9, 9, 10
   B. 5, 4, 2, 1, 6, 5, 3, 2, 4, 2, 5, 5, 2

2. For each distribution of scores, 1) compile a simple frequency distribution, and 2) identify the shape of the distribution of skew, if any.
   A. 9, 11, 12, 10, 12, 11, 8, 12, 10, 11, 12
   B. 8, 7, 7, 9, 5, 7, 7, 8, 6, 6, 7, 7

3. A small group of people in a college town set out to promote greater use of bicycles. One member of the group was eager to measure any progress. Before any promotion activity, she assessed five different modes of transportation by asking people how they got to work or school that morning. Responses were scored as auto---0, bicycle---1, motorcycle---2,

walk---3, bus---4. Arrange the scores into an appropriate frequency distribution and graph it. Write a sentence or two explaining what your analysis shows.

4	1	0	0	3	0	2	0	4	0
3	1	0	4	0	0	0	2	0	0
0	0	2	0	0	4	0	0	2	0
1	0	4	0	3	0	0	4	0	2

4. The numbers in this problem are weights in pounds of Americans aged 20-29 (http://usmilitary.about.com/library/milinfo/blcgweightmale.htm, retrieved, April 27, 2004). Compile one grouped frequency distribution for males and another for females. In both distributions use $i = 9$. For men the highest class interval is 237-245 pounds. For women the highest class interval is 217-225 pounds. Graph the men's weights using a histogram and the women's weights using a frequency polygon.

Men:

160	177	132	195	175	157	217	168	168	150
164	172	200	148	122	184	190	130	140	172
181	231	150	178	112	170	161	125	244	165
211	154	137	182	190					

Women:

140	152	129	135	118	159	134	114	146	172
162	132	138	101	140	164	124	123	201	133
124	132	168	154	121	95	142	130	218	151
110	136	191	128	118					

5. The American Psychological Association (*Graduate Study in Psychology,* 2004) publishes a book describing various graduate programs around the country. A random sample of GRE (Graduate Record Exam) scores for admission to clinical Ph.D. programs reveals the following numbers. Construct the appropriate distribution to display the data.

1240, 1210, 1259, 1260, 1225, 1268, 1190, 1150, 1176, 1390, 1150, 1235

CHAPTER 3

Central Tendency and Variability

Summary_____

This chapter covers two very important characteristics of distributions: *measures of central tendency* and *variability*. You have experience with the concepts of central tendency and variability even if you haven't studied the *mean* and *standard deviation* before. Calculating and interpreting measures of central tendency and variability such as the mean, median, mode, standard deviation, range, interquartile range, and variance gives you a quantitative way to express some familiar ideas.

Expressing ideas quantitatively can be very powerful. You already have a good bit of experience with this; for years you have used the *mean* when you want to get across the concept of "the typical member of the group." Other measures of central tendency are the *median* and the *mode*.

The mean is usually the preferred measure of central tendency, but it should not be used if a class interval is open ended, if the observations are nominal or ordinal data, or if the distribution is severely skewed. Nominal data limit you to the mode. Ordinal data limit you to the median and the mode.

The *median* and the *mode* are used less frequently than the mean. The median is the middlemost score of a rank ordered distribution. It is the score that corresponds to the 50th percentile. The median is in the appropriate measure of central tendency for skewed distributions.

The mode is the score that occurs most frequently. Some distributions have no modes and some have more than one mode. The mode is more informative when combined with the percentage of times that it occurs in the distribution.

Two mathematical characteristics of the mean are referred to later in the text. If you do not feel comfortable with the expressions $\Sigma(X - \overline{X}) = 0$ and $\Sigma(X - \overline{X})^2$ is a minimum, you should make up a small set of data and perform the operations that

Chapter 3

the formulas describe. Then, be alert for these ideas when they turn up in Chapter 4 and Chapter 5.

Calculating a weighted mean is easy. Recognizing when you can work from the individual means and when you have to calculate the overall sum of X takes practice. Some of the problems that follow give you that practice.

The first quantitative measure of variability in this chapter is the *range*, a simple and easily calculated statistic. The range is simply the numerical distance between the highest and lowest scores.

The *interquartile range* (IQR) gives you the scores in the distribution that are the middle 50 percent of the distribution. The IQR is the 75th percentile minus the 25th percentile. A location value (.25 × N) allows you to find the 75th percentile (by working from the top of the distribution) and the 25th percentile (by working from the bottom of the distribution).

Another important statistic is the *standard deviation.* The standard deviation tells you the average amount that scores differ from the mean. After studying the standard deviation in this chapter and again in Chapter 6, you will find it a powerful and accurate way to express the concept of variability.

The sections on the standard deviation show two ways to arrange the arithmetic—the *deviation-score* method and the *raw-score* method. The principal reason for learning the deviation-score method is that it gives you direct insight into the underlying workings of the standard deviation. However, a raw-score formula and a calculator produce more accurate answers more quickly. Raw-score formulas are given for *unorganized data* and for *frequency distributions.*

In the order of importance in the textbook, the three standard deviations are:

1. ŝ standard deviation of a sample, used to estimate σ ($N - 1$ in denominator)
2. σ standard deviation of a population (N in denominator)
3. S standard deviation of a sample is used when there is no interest in generalizing from the sample to its population. (N in denominator)

Chapter 3

Choosing among these three standard deviation depends on how the data were gathered (was sampling used?) and the purpose of the data gathering (generalization?).

Bars that extend one standard deviation can be added to a bar graph of means. Standard deviation bars indicate the spread of scores in the sample.

If the issue of N or $N - 1$ in the formula for a standard deviation has you shaking your head (sideways), I recommend that you work the exercise described in the footnote of the section, " as an estimate of σ" in the textbook.

The *variance* gets two short paragraphs in the text, which is not representative of its importance in the overall field of statistics. You will learn more about variance in Chapters 10, 11, and 12. As a *descriptive index* of variability, however, the variance is not nearly as useful as its square root, the standard deviation.

Multiple-Choice Questions _____

1. Which of the following words could legitimately fit into this sentence: "That simple frequency distribution has two _____, 13 and 18."
   - (1) means;
   - (2) medians;
   - (3) modes;
   - (4) all of the above.

2. Your text noted which of the following as a characteristic of the mean?
   - (1) The sum of the results of squaring the difference between each score and the mean is a minimum;
   - (2) The sum of the results of squaring the difference between each score and the mean is zero;
   - (3) Both (1) and (2);
   - (4) Neither (1) nor (2).

Chapter 3

3. For our study of driving habits, we recorded the speed of every fifth vehicle on Drury Lane. Nearly every car traveled right at the speed limit or a little over, but there were some that were 10 mph under, even fewer at 20 mph under, and one care that crept by at just 15 mph. On the basis of the central tendency calculations on our data, we drew conclusions about all drivers on this stretch of road. The proper central tendency value calculated from these data is the
   - (1) population median;
   - • (2) sample median;
   - ✗ (3) population mean (μ);
   - (4) sample mean ($\overline{X}$).

4. The mean temperature for January was 30°. In February the mean was 25° and for March the mean was 35°. The weighted mean for these three months is

   $$\frac{31(30) + 28(25) + 31(35)}{31 + 28 + 31} = 30.117$$

   - (1) 30°;
   - • (2) greater than 30°;
   - (3) less than 30°.

5. The standard deviation that estimates a population standard deviation from calculations on a sample is
   - (1) σ;
   - • (2) $\hat{s}$;
   - (3) S.

6. Two distributions that have the same mean must have the same
   - (1) range;
   - (2) standard deviation;
   - (3) variance;
   - • (4) none of the above.

7. Which of the following is (are) *not* mathematically possible if only one distribution is being considered?
   - • (1) range = $\hat{s}$;
   - (2) range = $\overline{X}$;
   - (3) range = μ;
   - (4) all of the above.

Chapter 3

8. You will get a negative number as a standard deviation
   (1) when all scores are negative;
   (2) when the mean of the scores is negative;
   (3) either (1) or (2) is sufficient;
   • (4) under no circumstances---standard deviations are *always* positive numbers.

9. An experimenter was interested in the variability of SAT scores in the new freshman class at her university. She obtained all the scores from the registrar. She should compute
   ✗ (1) σ;
   (2) $\hat{s}$;
   • (3) S;
   (4) the 50th percentile.

10. The standard deviation of the IQ's of students at a high school for the gifted and talented is _____ the standard deviation of IQ's of students at a high school that accepts everyone in its district.
    • (1) less than;
    (2) greater than;
    ✗ (3) equal to.

11. Which of the following distributions is the most variable?
    (1) 1, 2, 3;
    (2) 8, 9, 10;
    • (3) 1, 3, 5;
    (4) All of the above are equally variable.

12. Choose the statement that is true, according to your text.
    (1) The pay for people in management is more variable than the pay for those in sales;
    • (2) $\hat{s}$ is a biased estimate of σ;
    ✗ (3) In reaching puberty, males are more variable than females;
    (4) All of the above are true.

22

Chapter 3

13. The interquartile range always
    - (1) is one-fourth of the range;
    - (2) becomes larger if more observations are added;
    - (3) contains 50 percent of the frequencies;
    - (4) all of the above.

14. For a set of scores, the sum of the deviation scores will be zero
    - (1) when half the scores are negative;
    - (2) when the mean is zero;
    - (3) only when the standard deviation is zero;
    - (4) always.

15. From all the employees in a company, a small group was selected to participate in a study of employee satisfaction. The results of the study were to be generalized to all the employees of the company. To find the variability in satisfaction, the investigator should compute
    - (1) μ;
    - (2) S;
    - (3) $\hat{s}$;
    - (4) σ.

16. For a sample of 100 or fewer, the standard deviation could be about _____ the range. (Be careful on this one.)
    - (1) 2 times;
    - (2) 5 times;
    - (3) 2-5 times;
    - (4) one fourth.

Chapter 3

17. On the first test of material on dinosaurs, a class of sixth graders had a mean score of 36 with S = 12. The teacher was disappointed and assigned six pages of homework on dinosaurs and scheduled a second test. The top one-fourth of the class studied the extra material and did even better on the second test. The other three-fourths ignored the material and made the same scores as before. Pick the mean and standard deviation that might be found, given the description.
    (1) $\bar{X}$ = 36, S = 12;
    (2) $\bar{X}$ = 36, S = 18;
  • (3) $\bar{X}$ = 42, S = 18;
    (4) $\bar{X}$ = 42, S = 12.

18. Which of the following may be a negative number?
    ✝ (1) range;
    (2) variance;
  • (3) deviation score; *individual score*
    (4) both (2) and (3).

19. Suppose you had a sample and you wanted to draw conclusions about the variability of a population. You should calculate
  • (1) ŝ;
    (2) S;
    (3) IQR;
    (4) the range.

20. The variance is _____ the standard deviation.
    (1) the sum of;
  • (2) the square of;
    (3) the square root of;
    (4) twice as large as.

Short-Answer Questions_____

1. Your text described three situations in which the median should be used rather than the mean. List them.
    extreme scores, open ended scores, skewness

Chapter 3

2. Our company has three divisions. Based on our capital invested, Division A made $.10 per dollar, Division B made $.20 per dollar and Division C made $.25 per dollar. Therefore, the profit for the company was $.1833 per dollar invested. Do you agree with this conclusion? Why or why not?

3. This is a thought question about the distribution of class sizes in a typical college. There are usually a few courses, typically at the first-year level, that have large enrollments. Most of a college's courses, however, are at the junior and senior level, and in these courses, enrollments are much smaller. Suppose the mean class size in such a college is 23. Is the median larger or smaller?

4. The question is, "How can I buy groceries cheaply *and* efficiently?" Suppose there are four equally convenient supermarkets and they all place advertisements in the newspaper on Wednesday. From these advertisements you have noted the prices for Red Delicious apples (per pound), skim milk (per gallon), and Froot Loops cereal (per 12 oz). From your notes you have calculated the standard deviations of the prices of each item. The results are: Apples-----$.10, Milk-----$.02, Cereal-----$.01. Now suppose you are going to buy the three items and you want to do it cheaply and efficiently. You have this week's ads. What do you do?

5. Tell what each of the three types of standard deviations is used for; that is, which are used on samples, and which are used on populations.

Problems _____

1. "Count Avogadro, would you give us your number?" asked a pleasant voice on the phone. "This is your bank and we need your number," the voice continued. Suspecting a scam, Avogadro said, "My number? Here are several: 6.2, 5.8, 5.9, 6.1, and 6.1. Use them to find my number."
   > Find the mean, median and mode of the numbers. (To get a psychological bonus from this problem, identify the number that Avogadro might claim as his).

mean = 6.02
median = 6.1
mode = 6.1

Chapter 3

2. From each distribution of scores, find the mean, median and mode
   A. 9, 10, 9, 9, 11, 9, 10, 9, 9, 10 $\bar{x} = 9.5, mdn = 9, mode = 9$
   B. 5, 4, 2, 1, 6, 5, 3, 2, 4, 2, 5, 5, 2 $\bar{x} = 3.54, mdn = 4, mode = 2+5$
   C. 9, 11, 12, 10, 12, 11, 8, 12, 10, 11, 12 $\bar{x} = 10.73, mdn = 11, mode = 12$
   D. 8, 7, 7, 9, 5, 7, 7, 8, 6, 6, 7, 7 $\bar{x} = 7, mdn = 7, mode = 7$

3. A Likert scale is a standardized method of collecting opinions. A statement is presented such as, "Social security is not important as a means of income for the elderly." Responses are limited to 5 choices anchored by "strongly agree" (scored 1) to "strongly disagree" (scored 5). "No opinion" is scored 3. The two frequency distributions that follow show the responses of College Students and Older Adults to the statement above. For each distribution, find the mean, median and mode.

College Students:
$\bar{X} = 3.75$
mdn = 4
mode = 4 +5

Adults:
$\bar{X} = 2.27$
mdn = 2
mode = 1

College Students	f	fx	Older Adults	f	fx
5	4	20	5	2	10
4	4	16	4	1	4
3 N=12	2	6	3 N=15	2	6
2	1	2	2	4	8
1	1	1	1	6	6
		$\Sigma fx = 45$			$\Sigma fx = 34$

4. The numbers below are somewhat representative of human birthweights in 1984 and 2004. For each year, find the mean, median and mode.

1984:
$\bar{X} = 7.13$
mdn = 7
mode = 7

2004:
$\bar{X} = 7.57$
mdn = 7.5
mode = 7

1984 Weight (lbs.)	f	fx	2004 Weights (lbs.)	f	fx
5	1	5	5	1	5
6 N=15	3	18	6	2	12
7	7	49	7 N=14	4	28
8	2	16	8	3	24
9	1	9	9	3	27
10	1	10	10	1	10
		$\Sigma fx = 107$			$\Sigma fx = 106$

Chapter 3

5. For the weight data of 20-29 year old Americans (Problem 4 in Chapter 2), find the range and interquartile range.

6. The following data are representative of the age (in months) at which 90 percent of babies first stand without support (Berk, 2004). Compile appropriate statistics, and write a paragraph report to parents about the age they can expect their baby to stand. A report that explains both the typical case and variability is needed.

mean = 11.71
man = 11
mode = 11

$\hat{S} = \sqrt{\dfrac{5319 - \dfrac{198025}{38}}{37}} = 1.71$

Age (months)		f	fx	fx^2
16		1	16	256
15	N=38	2	30	450
14		3	42	588
13		— 5	65	845
12		7	84	1008
11		10	110	1210
10		— 8	80	800
9		2	18	162

$\Sigma fx = 445$ $\Sigma fx^2 = 5319$

$(\Sigma fx)^2 = 198025$

7. The data you analyzed in Problem 2b in Chapter 2 show the numbers of digits a person can hear and then repeat without error (memory span scores). Treat those data as a population and use the deviation-score method to find σ. Also, calculate the range and interquartile range.

8. The data in Problem 3 above reveal the opinions of college students and older adults on the value of social security. Find the range, IQR, and $\hat{s}$.

range = 16 - 9 = 7   IQR = 13 - 10 = 3 $\hat{s} = 1.71$

9. The Clock Test is a technique for studying human vigilance. In the Clock Test, a hand moves regularly at one step per second, but sometimes, at random intervals, it jumps two steps. The participant's task is to notice the two-step jumps and press a button. The numbers that follow are the percentages of two-step jumps that were missed by 5 participants during the first 15 minutes of a two-hour watch. Estimate the size of the standard deviation. Calculate an estimate of σ and σ^2 using the raw-score method.

11   8   17   10   14

10. In the Clock Test experiment described in Problem 9, the percentages of missed jumps during the *last* 15 minutes of the two-hour watch are much higher than the first 15 minutes. Estimate the standard deviation of the scores that follow. Calculate estimates of σ and σ^2. Using this answer and your answer from Problem 6, write a sentence about the effect of two hours of vigilance on variability.

25	12	38	21	29

CHAPTER 4

Other Descriptive Statistics

Summary _____

This chapter covers *z* scores, box plots, the effect size index and the Descriptive Statistics Report. The first three are descriptive statistics that combine two or more simpler descriptive statistics. A Descriptive Statistics Report presents several statistics about a data set as well as an explanation of what the statistics mean.

A *z score* (also called a standardized score) is the difference between a raw score and the mean of the distribution divided by the standard deviation of the distribution. z scores are used to compare the relative positions of scores within one distribution or the relative position of scores in different distributions, and allow us to make a comparison between different populations by using a common metric. Typically, descriptive statistic *z* scores range from –3 to +3. As an inferential statistic, however, *z* scores can occur outside this range.

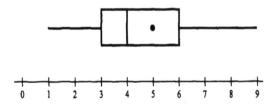

There are two parts to a *boxplot* (see above). The first, a horizontal axis, shows all the scores in a distribution. The second, a box with whiskers, has elements that correspond to various descriptive statistics. Elements of the box and whiskers are aligned over their corresponding values on the horizontal axis. Within the box, the mean is indicated by a dot; the median by a vertical line. The width of the box from left to right spans the interquartile range. The ends of the whiskers are over the lowest and highest scores in the distribution. The skew of the distribution can be determined by the relation of the mean to the median and also by comparing the relative length of the whiskers.

Chapter 4

The *effect size index* (*d*) describes the amount of difference between two distributions. Effect size estimates are often used to help researchers understand the amount of influence the independent variable has on the dependent variable. To find *d*, divide the difference between the means of the two distributions by a standard deviation. Values of *d* are judged by a convention that assigns the descriptors, "small", "medium", and "large" to values of .20, .50, and .80, respectively. Adjectives are used to modify the descriptors for intermediate and extreme values of *d*.

For an experiment that compares two groups, a *Descriptive Statistics Report* gives the reader an overview of the results. It consists of a boxplot and a narrative. A Descriptive Statistics Report typically reports means, medians, ranges, IQR's, skew, and an effect size index. The major purpose of a Descriptive Statistics Report is to explain to the reader what an experiment revealed.

Multiple-Choice Questions _____

1. A *z* score conveys the
   (1) central tendency of a distribution;
   (2) variability of a distribution;
   ◦ (3) relative position of an individual;
   (4) all of the above.

2. A *z* score close to zero indicates
   (1) a raw score near the bottom of the distribution;
   • (2) a raw score close to the mean;
   (3) a distribution with little variability;
   (4) a distribution that is quite variable.

3. A *z* score of 2.5 indicates
   (1) a raw score close to the mean;
   (2) a raw score that is much smaller than the mean;
   • (3) a raw score that is much larger than the mean;
   (4) a raw score that is 2.5 times larger than the mean .

Chapter 4

4. The advantage of using *z* scores over using raw scores is that z scores allow you to
    - (1) compare a score in one distribution to a score in another;
    - (2) understand the relationship of a score to the mean;
    - • (3) both (1) and (2);
    - (4) neither (1) nor (2).

5. For four years in a row at the annual Late 90's Video Game Contest, a different entrant won the contest. The field of contestants was different each year. Each year's winners, amount of time they were able to play, and contest statistics are shown. Who was the overall winner?
    - (1) Year 1: Zach, 32 hours; $\overline{X}$ = 28 hours; S = 2 hours; $\frac{32-28}{2} = 2$
    - • (2) Year 2: Slater, 34 hours; $\overline{X}$ = 29 hours; S = 2 hours; $\frac{34-29}{2} = 2.5$
    - (3) Year 3: Screech, 36 hours; $\overline{X}$ = 30 hours; S = 6 hours; $\frac{36-30}{6} = 1$
    - (4) Year 4: Lisa, 28 hours; $\overline{X}$ = 24 hours; S = 3 hours. $\frac{28-24}{3} = 1.33$

6. The number of descriptive statistics conveyed by a boxplot is
    - (1) one;
    - (2) two;
    - (3) three;
    - (4) more than three.

7. A boxplot of a negatively skewed distribution has a whisker over the lower scores that is
    _____ than the whisker over the higher scores.
    - (1) longer;
    - (2) shorter;
    - (3) unable to determine.

8. In a boxplot of a positively skewed distribution, the mean is
    - (1) greater than the median;
    - (2) less than the median;
    - (3) out of the interquartile box;
    - (4) in the middle of the interquartile box.

Chapter 4

9. To determine the range of a distribution using a boxplot, look at.
    (1) the difference between the dot and the line in the box;
    (2) the ends of the box;
    (3) the ends of the whiskers;
    (4) any of the above will work.

10. Ouliers (extreme scores) can be presented in a boxplot as points
    (1) within the box;
    (2) above the box;
    (3) below the box;
    (4) beyond the whiskers.

11. The measure of central tendency that is not presented in a boxplot is the
    (1) mean;
    (2) median;
    (3) mode;
    (4) all of the above.

12. The percent of frequencies covered by the box portion of a boxplot is
    (1) 100 percent;
    (2) 95 percent;
    (3) 50 percent;
    (4) 5 percent.

13. Group A's mean was a whopping 110, but it was exceeded by Group B's mean of 114. The effect size index in this contest was 0.20. The difference between the two groups should be described as
    (1) very large;
    (2) large;
    (3) medium;
    (4) small.

Chapter 4

14. From an effect size estimate of 0.70, you can determine that the means of the two groups are
    (1) identical;
    (2) different by 70 percent;
    (3) related to each other;
    (4) very different.

15. An effect size index is a measure of
    (1) the relative position of an individual;
    (2) the effectiveness of a Descriptive Statistics Report;
    (3) the accuracy of the calculations;
    (4) none of the above.

16. An effect size index is measure of
    (1) the size of the means of the two distributions;
    (2) the difference in the means of the two distributions;
    (3) the size of the standard deviations of the two distributions;
    (4) the size of the ranges of the two distributions.

17. An experiment compared two groups. The effect size index was just less than 1.00. The difference between the two groups is
    (1) large;
    (2) medium;
    (3) small;
    (4) very small.

18. The effect size estimate, *d,* is a useful measure because it
    (1) provides new information about the relationship between two groups;
    (2) shows the effect the independent variable has on the dependent variable;
    (3) it allows direct comparisons to other studies;
    (4) all are true.

Chapter 4

19. A Descriptive Statistics Report has information about
    (1) central tendency;
    (2) variability;
    (3) effect size index;
    (4) all of the above.

20. The purpose of a Descriptive Statistics Report is to
    (1) avoid arithmetic errors in reporting descriptive statistics;
    (2) present tables that show descriptive statistics;
    (3) explain the results of a two-group experiment;
    (4) present results without using graphs.

Short-Answer Questions_____

1. What does a z of 0 equal in a distribution of raw scores? *the mean*
2. Write from memory the d values that are considered small, medium, and large.
3. What descriptive statistics are presented in a boxplot?

Problems _____

1. For Problems 3b and 3 in Chapters 2 and 3, you analyzed data from a memory span study. Using those analyses, create a boxplot. Write an explanation of what the boxplot shows.

2. You analyzed the age at which babies are first able to stand alone in Chapter 3 (Problem 6). Create a boxplot using your analysis. Write an explanation for parents who understand boxplots.

3. For the data on weights of 20-29 year-old Americans, compose a boxplot, calculate the effect size index, and write a Descriptive Statistics Report. ($\overline{X}_{Men} = 180$ pounds; $\overline{X}_{Women} = 145$ pounds; $\sigma = 40$ pounds) Work from the grouped frequency distributions and statistics you calculated in Problems 4 and 7 in Chapters 2 and 3 respectively.

Chapter 4

4. Compose a boxplot, calculate the effect size index, and write a Descriptive Statistics Report for the 1984 and 2004 human birthweight data (Problem 4 in Chapter 3). Let $\sigma = 1.25$ pounds.

5. The question in this problem is the same as one in your text, "Just how different in cognitive ability are first and second born siblings?" Breland (1974) collected data on cognitive ability from National Merit Scholarship participants. For two children families, the mean of first-born children was 107.5; for second-born children, the mean was 105.5. The standard deviation was 21. Find the effect size index. Write a sentence of interpretation that incorporates the results described in the textbook problem.

6. The average score on an IQ test is 100, and the standard deviation is 15. What z score corresponds to raw scores of
   - a. 115 $+1$
   - b. 124 1.6
   - c. 97 $-.2$
   - d. 101 $.07$
   - e. 87 $-.87$

7. Assume the same characteristics of IQ scores as those given in Question 6. What raw score corresponds to z scores of
   - a. -.533 92.005
   - b. 1.40 121
   - c. 2.73 140.95
   - d. -1.93 71.05

CHAPTER 5

Correlation and Regression

Summary _____

Correlation and *regression* are two different statistical methods that are closely related mathematically. Both methods provide information about *bivariate distributions*. A bivariate distribution has two variables whose scores are logically paired.

Correlation and regression are used for different purposes. A correlation coefficient (symbolized as r), is used to describe the *degree* and the *direction* of a relationship between two variables. A regression equation is used to draw a *line of best fit* and to *predict scores* on one variable, if you have scores on the other variable. The textbook describes the simplest case for these two methods, the case which requires that the two variables have a *linear relationship*. You can make a visual check for linearity by constructing and examining a scatterplot of the two variables. This is a recurring theme in the text and the study guide; when in doubt, graph the data to gain insight into the nature of the relationship between variables.

The two most important names in this chapter are Francis Galton, who conceived the idea of a correlation statistic, and Karl Pearson, who developed the mathematics for calculating the correlation coefficient.

Your textbook gives two methods of arranging the arithmetic when you calculate r. If you choose to use the "blanched" (partially cooked) formula, be sure you (or your calculator) carry three or four decimal places in the calculations.

To summarize several of the characteristics of r and its interpretation:

a.   The *algebraic sign* of r gives the direction of the relationship. If the sign is positive, the relationship is direct (higher scores on one variable go with higher scores on the other variable). If the sign is negative, the relationship is inverse (higher scores on one variable go with lower scores on the other).

Chapter 5

b. The closer the absolute value of *r* is to 1.00, the stronger the relationship, and the more confidence you can put into a prediction made from a regression equation based on the data.

c. Positive coefficients are not "better" than negative coefficients.

d. r^2, the *coefficient of determination*, gives the proportion of variance the two variables have in common.

e. Correlation coefficients, no matter how large, *are not sufficient evidence to claim a causal relationship between two variables*.

f. Low correlations do not necessarily mean that there is no relationship between the two variables; *nonlinear relationships* and *truncated ranges* both produce spuriously (artificially) low correlation coefficients.

g. The *effect size index* for a correlation coefficient is the correlation coefficient itself. Depending on the reason that *r* was calculated, descriptive adjectives of *small, medium, and large* are appropriate for different values of *r*.

h. When the same measure is administered twice to the same subjects, a correlation coefficient of .80 or greater indicates that the measure is *reliable*.

Besides the Pearson product-moment correlation coefficient, which is used for *two quantitative variables*, other kinds of correlation coefficients are used when the relationship between variables is examined. Any correlation coefficient expresses the strength and direction of the relationship between variables.

A *regression equation*, $\hat{Y} = a + bX$, allows you to predict a value for *Y* for any value of *X*. The prediction will be more accurate when the relationship between *X* and *Y* is linear and the correlation coefficient is large.

To write a regression equation for a bivariate distribution, calculate values for the *two regression coefficients*, *a* and *b*. The regression coefficient, *a* is the *intercept* of the regression line with the *Y* axis, and the coefficient *b* is the slope of the regression line.

Chapter 5

A regression line can be presented as a graph, but its appearance will depend on the units used on the X and Y axes. Also, there are two regression lines for one set of bivariate data. The line that your calculations produce depends on which variable you designate as the Y variable.

Multiple-Choice Questions _____

1. To use the regression equation technique described in your text, you must have
    (1) a logical pairing of the scores on the two variables;
    (2) a linear relationship between the two variables;
  ◦ (3) both (1) and (2);
    (4) neither (1) nor (2).

2. Quantification is the idea that
    (1) all things can be counted;
    (2) all physical things can be counted;
    (3) the numerical representation of a phenomenon gives the most important picture;
  ◦ (4) a phenomenon can be better understood if its important parts are expressed as numbers.

3. A Pearson correlation coefficient is appropriate to describe which of the situations below?
  ◦ (1) As X increases, Y decreases by the same amount;
    (2) As X increases, Y goes up at first slowly and then faster;
    (3) As X increases, Y goes up at first and then goes down;
    (4) All of the above.

4. A correlation of -.88 between television viewing time and grades in high school is best understood as demonstrating that
    (1) as television viewing time increases, grades increase;
    (2) as television viewing time decreases, grades decrease;
  ◦ (3) as television viewing time increases, grades decrease;
    (4) both (1) and (2) are correct.

Chapter 5

5. Assume you conduct a study to evaluate the relationship between the amount of time a child is read to and reading ability at age 15. You find a correlation coefficient of .04. This correlation suggests
- (1) a very strong relationship; as reading to children increases, reading ability increases;
- (2) a very weak relationship; as reading to children increases, reading ability decreases slightly;
- (3) almost no relationship;
- (4) unable to tell without knowing the number of participants.

6. A linear relationship is described by which of the statements below?
- (1) The two variables are paired in some logical fashion;
- (2) For every one-point increase in one variable, you get a four-point increase in the other variable;
- (3) Both (1) and (2);
- (4) Neither (1) nor (2).

7. A Pearson product-moment correlation coefficient can be used to express the degree of relationship for which situation(s) below?
- (1) A little anxiety produces poor results, a moderate amount produces good results, and a high level of anxiety produces poor results;
- (2) Early in training each trial helps only a little, but as training progresses, each trial causes larger and larger gain;
- (3) For every extra year of growth in a pine forest, you can expect an increase of 10,000 board feet;
- (4) All of the above.

8. Which of the following statements is (are) true?
- (1) Correlations range from -1 to +1;
- (2) Correlations show causal relationships;
- (3) Correlations allow us to evaluate the strength of a relationship;
- (4) Both (1) and (3) are correct.

Chapter 5

9. Psychologists have demonstrated that number of hours spent in class is correlated with grades in that class. The correlation between number of hours in class and grades is

+ (1) positive;
   (2) negative;
   (3) zero;
   • (4) not determinable from the information given.

10. Identify the incorrect statement.
   (1) A negative correlation is obtained when high scores on X go with low scores on Y and low scores on X go with high scores on Y;
   (2) A positive correlation is obtained when high scores on X go with high scores on Y;
   (3) A zero correlation is obtained when high scores on X go with both high and low scores on Y and low scores on X go with both high and low scores on Y;
   ⊜ (4) None of the above.

11. The coefficient of determination allows you to
   ⊜ (1) determine the variance two variables have in common;
   (2) draw cause-and-effect statements;
   (3) predict X scores, given Y scores;
   (4) quickly determine the regression coefficients.

12. Given a correlation coefficient of zero, which conclusion is correct?
   ⊜ (1) There is no relationship between the two variables;
   (2) A correlation coefficient is not proper for the data;
   (3) Correlation coefficients of zero cannot be interpreted;
   (4) All of the above.

13. The least squares method of finding a formula for a straight line
   ✗ (1) produces a slope and an intercept;
   (2) makes the error in prediction a minimal amount;
   (3) was championed by Karl Pearson;
   • (4) all of the above.

Chapter 5

14. Pearson product-moment correlation coefficients can be used to establish the degree of relationship
    - (1) even if the two variables are measuring different things;
    - (2) even if the full ranges of the two variables are not included in the data;
    - (3) even though the relationship is not linear;
    - (4) all of the above.

15. The regression coefficient, a, is most clearly related to
    - (1) the angle the regression line makes with the X axis;
    - (2) the place the regression line crosses the Y axis;
    - (3) the Y score predicted for the X score that is the mean of the X distribution;
    - (4) the absolute size of the correlation coefficient.

16. One reason for a small correlation might be
    - (1) truncated range;
    - (2) nonlinear relationship;
    - (3) neither (1) nor (2);
    - (4) both (1) and (2).

17. Suppose you know that the regression coefficients for the line that predicts the number of offspring of children from the number of offspring of the maternal grandmother are $a = 10$, $b = -1.0$. Knowing this, you can conclude that the correlation coefficient for these data is
    - (1) positive;
    - (2) negative;
    - (3) perfect;
    - (4) none of the above.

18. Error in a regression analysis is defined as
    - (1) $\hat{Y}$;
    - (2) $Y - \hat{Y}$;
    - (3) $\hat{Y} - Y$;
    - (4) $(Y - \hat{Y})^2$.

Chapter 5

19. Suppose you had the exam scores on the first hour exam for 100 general psychology students. A correlation coefficient could be calculated if the scores were divided according to the variable_____.
    (1) gender-------males and females;
    (2) where a person sits in the class-------front or back;
    (3) both (1) and (2);
    (4) neither (1) nor (2).

20. The difference between correlation coefficients and regression equations is that correlation coefficients
    (1) allows us to infer causation; regression equations do not;
    (2) allows prediction of scores; regression equations do not;
    (3) give the relationship between two variables; regression equations predict scores;
    (4) they are the same procedure.

Short-Answer Questions_____

1. "The self-confidence of that group of recruits is negatively correlated with their success in the obstacle course." Tell what this statement means.

2. Describe the statistical method of regression. Tell what it is good for and what its limitations are.

3. A study of 4138 students in 25 law schools found a correlation coefficient of .36 between first-year law school grades and scores on the Law School Admission Test. Interpret the meaning of this correlation.

4. Assume that the correlation between SAT scores and GPA in college is .35. Interpret the meaning of this correlation.

5. Some personality assessments ask you to identify items in a series that are "like you" or "not like you." Examples are items such as, "I am a hard worker" or "I don't care what happens to my neighbors." One of the problems facing psychologists who are developing personality assessments is that the items differ in their social desirability. (The two items above are good examples). Asking people to rate the

Chapter 5

social desirability of each item on a scale of 1 to 9 is a common way to find out about items.

Imagine that 20 nuns rate a set of 100 items. For each item a mean is calculated. Now imagine that 20 convicted child molesters rate the same set of items. Again a mean is calculated for each item. Stop a moment and estimate the correlation coefficient for the two sets of ratings (positive or negative, high or low). Based on other studies, the correlation coefficient between the two sets of ratings will be about .90.

a. What is the N that the correlation is based on?

b. Write a sentence that explains the meaning of this correlation coefficient.

Problems _____

1. The idea of using tests to predict who will do well in college began to emerge around 1900. Many (including Galton) assumed that people with quick reaction times and keen sensory abilities would be quick thinkers with keen intellects (who would, of course, make good grades). James McKeen Cattell at Columbia University gathered data on this assumption. The summary statistics below are representative of his findings, as reported by Clark Wissler. (See Sokal [1982] for an overview.)

Sensory Ability Score $\quad\quad$ Grade Point Average

$\quad\quad \Sigma X = 3500 \quad\quad\quad\quad\quad\quad \Sigma Y = 115$

$\quad\quad \Sigma X^2 = 250,000 \quad\quad\quad\quad \Sigma Y^2 = 289$

$\quad\quad\quad\quad \Sigma XY = 8084$

$\quad\quad\quad\quad N = 50$

a. Calculate the correlation coefficient between sensory ability and freshman grade point average.

b. Write the regression equation that predicts GPA.

c. Predict the GPA of a person with a sensory ability score of 100.

d. Tell in words how much faith you have that a person with a sensory ability score of 100 would have the GPA you predicted.

Chapter 5

2. Does reading improve vocabulary? An elementary school teacher thought so. To prove the case, he gathered data for 12 children on time spent reading. Each child's time score in minutes matched with his or her vocabulary score. Summary statistics follow.

Reading Time
$\Sigma X = 252$
$\Sigma X^2 = 7644$

Vocabulary Score
$\Sigma Y = 204$
$\Sigma Y^2 = 3607$

$\Sigma XY = 4787$
$N = 12$

    a. Find the correlation coefficient between reading time and vocabulary score.
    b. Write the regression equation that predicts vocabulary score.
    c. Predict the vocabulary score of a child with a reading time of 50 minutes.
    d. Tell in words how much faith you have that a child with a reading time of 50 minutes would have the vocabulary score you predicted.
    e. Comment on this conclusion: "These data show that reading improves vocabulary."

3. Is creativity related to humor? Each student in this data set has a score on a test of creativity and a score based on the number of puns produced while looking at a list of "wise sayings." Draw a scatterplot and find the correlation coefficient and the coefficient of determination. Write the regression equation and plot the line on your scatterplot. Write an explanation of what your analysis shows. Predict the number of puns for a student whose creativity test score was 93.

Student	Creativity Test Score	Number of Puns	X^2	Y^2	XY
1	60	28	3600	784	1680
2	57	32	3249	1024	1824
3	52	24	2704	576	1248
4	46	16	2116	256	736
5	41	21	1681	441	861
6	38	14	1444	196	532
7	32	18	1024	324	576
8	29	11	841	121	319
9	25	9	625	81	225
10	19	12	361	144	228

N=10

$\Sigma X = 399$
$\bar{X} = 39.9$

$\Sigma Y = 185$
$\bar{Y} = 18.5$

$\Sigma Y^2 = 3947$ $\Sigma XY = 8229$

$\Sigma X^2 = 17645$

Chapter 5

4. Studies of conformity require a participant to make a judgment about a stimulus. Afterward, pressure to conform is applied (which might be that everyone else gives a judgment that differs from the participant's judgment). The stimulus (or one similar) is presented again. The dependent variable is the amount of change in the participant's judgment.

Each subject below participated in two conformity sessions. The first session involved estimates of distance; the second involved value judgments about the degree of truth in ten controversial statements. Begin by looking at the data and making a judgment about the size and direction of the correlation coefficient. (To get a feeling for being a participant in conformity research, share your estimate with fellow class members, who then share theirs with you.) Calculate an r and write an interpretation. Write the regression equation for these data, treating the value judgments as the Y variable.

Participant	Distance Judgments	Value Judgments	X^2	Y^2	XY
1	8	1	64	1	8
2	4	2	16	4	8
3	7	0	49	0	0
4	9	3	81	9	27
5	3	1	9	1	3
6	0	2	0	4	0
7	4	0	16	0	0

$N=7$

$\bar{X}=5$ $\bar{Y}=1.29$

$\Sigma X = 35$ $\Sigma Y = 9$ $\Sigma X^2 = 235$ $\Sigma Y^2 19$ $\Sigma XY = 46$

5. Assume you are interested in predicting the GPA of college students by knowing their high school class rank. From records, you are able to obtain the high school ranks of 8 students, and they you find those students' college GPAs. From these data, create a scatter plot, write a regression equation and draw your line on the plot. Assume you have a student with a high school rank of 4. Predict the student's college GPA.

Chapter 5

Participant	High School Rank	X^2	College GPA	Y^2	XY
1	28	784	3.16	9.99	88.48
2	4	16	2.55	6.50	10.2
3	47	2209	3.10	9.61	145.7
4	19	361	3.97	15.76	75.43
5	43	1849	1.84	3.39	79.12
6	50	2500	2.99	8.94	149.5
7	34	1156	2.07	4.28	70.38
8	21	441	3.01	9.06	63.21

$N = 8$

$$\Sigma x = 246 \quad \Sigma x^2 = 9316 \qquad \Sigma Y = 22.69 \qquad \Sigma Y^2 = 67.53 \quad \Sigma XY = 682.02$$

$$\bar{x} = 30.75 \qquad \bar{Y} = 2.84$$

$$r = \frac{\frac{\Sigma XY}{N} - \bar{x}\bar{Y}}{S_x S_y} = \frac{\frac{682.02}{8} - (30.75)(2.84)}{(14.8)(.613)} = -.229$$

$$S_x = \sqrt{\frac{\Sigma X^2}{N} - (\bar{x})^2} = \sqrt{\frac{9316}{8} - (30.75)^2} = 14.8$$

$$S_y = \sqrt{\frac{\Sigma Y^2}{N} - (\bar{Y})^2} = \sqrt{\frac{67.53}{8} - (2.84)^2} = .613$$

$$b = r\frac{S_y}{S_x} = (-.229)\frac{.613}{14.8} = -.009$$

$$a = \bar{Y} - b\bar{x} = 2.84 - (-0.009)(30.75) = 3.12$$

$$\hat{Y} = a + bx$$
$$\hat{Y} = 3.12 - 0.009X$$
$$\text{if } X = 4$$
$$\hat{Y} = 3.16$$

CHAPTER 6

Theoretical Distributions Including
The Normal Distribution

Summary _____

Empirical distributions are frequency distributions of observed scores. *Theoretical distributions* are distributions based on logic or mathematical formulas. The current chapter focuses on finding probabilities by using theoretical distributions and then using those probabilities to answer questions about empirical distributions.

The concept of probability is central to understanding inferential statistics. To find the empirical probability of an event, form a ratio with successes in the numerator and the total of successes and failures in the denominator. To find the theoretical probability of an event, determine the proportion of a theoretical curve that corresponds to the events in question.

Major portions of this chapter are about using theoretical curves to find probabilities of events. With the theoretical curves in this chapter, the probability of an event is equal to the proportion of the curve that corresponds to that event.

Three different theoretical distributions are described – *rectangle distributions* (for example, playing cards), *binomial distributions* (for example, flipping a coin) and the *normal distribution* (lots of measures in the social sciences are normally distributed). Each distribution allows us to know the probability of events (or sets of events).

The normal curve is a bell-shaped distribution (sometimes called the "bell curve"). The unit of measurement on the X axis is the *z score*, which extends from approximately –3 on the left to 0 in the middle to approximately +3 on the right side. The points marked on the curve in between are at *z* scores of –1 and +1.

Chapter 6

Any empirical distribution that is not normally distributed can be converted to a normal distribution using z scores $\left(\dfrac{X - \mu}{\sigma}\right)$. Using z scores and the table of proportions of the normal curve, you can find:

1. the proportion of the empirical distribution that is beyond a particular score
2. the proportion of the empirical distribution that is between two particular scores
3. a particular score that separates out a proportion of the curve
4. two particular scores that encompass a given proportion of the curve
5. the number of cases with particular scores
6. the number of cases within a particular proportion of the curve

Drawing a picture of a theoretical distribution is highly recommended (even if the drawing doesn't quite look like the one in your book). Drawing a curve and labeling the known and unknown will help you understand the problem more completely. Once you understand it, finding an answer involves only a little algebra. Of course, to write an interpretation, it is necessary that you understand the problem.

Multiple-Choice Questions _____

1. The difference between an empirical distribution and a theoretical distribution is that a theoretical distribution
    (1) is based on many more observations;
    (2) is theory and cannot be used;
    (3) is based on mathematics and logic;
    (4) is based solely on observations.

2. Which of the following is an empirical distribution?
    (1) the given names and their frequencies of all high school graduates in the United States for the year 2005;
    (2) the scores expected from an infinite number of throws of one die;
    (3) the normal distribution in Table C in your text;
    (4) all of the above.

Chapter 6

3. To use the theoretical normal curve, which of the following things must be known about the population?
    (1) mean;
    (2) standard deviation;
    (3) the form of the distribution;
    ● (4) all of the above.

4. The term *normal distribution* was adopted because
    (1) the results were found only with normal, healthy individuals;
    (2) Sir Francis Normal was the first to write the equation for the curve;
    (3) results were first applied by teachers who had been trained in teachers' colleges, which, in those days, were called Normal Schools;
    ● (4) none of the above.

5. The area under the curve of a standard normal distribution is
    (1) dependent on the number of frequencies;
    (2) dependent on the size of the mean;
    ● (3) 1.00;
    (4) none of the above.

6. The theoretical normal curve has a mean equal to _____ and a standard deviation equal to _____.
    (1) 1.00, 0.00;
    ● (2) 0.00, 1.00;
    (3) 1.00, 1.00;
    (4) 1.00, the standard deviation of the population.

7. If you were given one z score from a population of measurements and nothing else, you could determine
    (1) the mean of the population;
    (2) the standard deviation of the population;
    (3) both (1) and (2)
    ● (4) neither (1) nor (2)

Chapter 6

8. .4332 of the normal curve lies between μ and 1.5σ. The proportion between μ and .75σ is
    - (1) .8664
    - ✶ (2) .2166
    - (3) .0668
    - (4) not determinable from the information given.

9. If a normal distribution of empirical scores is converted to a distribution of z scores,
    - (1) the new mean will be zero;
    - (2) the new standard deviation will be 1;
    - (3) both (1) and (2)
    - (4) neither (1) or (2)

10. Which of the following is a theoretical distribution?
    - (1) Your statistics professor stayed in the residence hall one Friday night and flipped a coin 10,000 times. The number of heads and tails was recorded.
    - (2) The price of every house sold in the last five years in Hampden County was obtained from courthouse records.
    - (3) The number of persons who arrived late was recorded every time a statistics course met during the semester.
    - (4) None of the above.

11. Bud and Lou were arguing about scores on the Ace Slap-Stick Comedy Test. The scores are distributed normally with a mean of 50. They agreed that 10% of the population had scores of 60 or better (and they were correct on this). Bud also claimed that 10% of the population had scores of 40 or below.
    - (1) Bud is correct;
    - (2) Bud is correct, but only because each score point is worth one percentage point;
    - (3) Bud is mistaken;
    - (4) More information is necessary before a decision can be made.

Chapter 6

12. Continuing the example of the Ace Slap-Stick Comedy Test, Bud claimed that, because 10% of the population had scores of 60 or better, which is 10 points from the mean, 5% must have had scores of 70 or better, because doubling the score distance always halves the percentage.
    - (1) Bud is correct;
    - (2) Bud is mistaken;
    - (3) More information is necessary before a decision can be made.

13. Suppose the mean of a particular normal distribution is 3.95. The median of this distribution will be
    - (1) larger than 3.95;
    - (2) smaller than 3.95;
    - (3) 3.95;
    - (4) not determinable from the information given.

14. Suppose that if K should occur, it will be called a success. If j should occur, it will be called a failure. The ratio $\dfrac{k}{j}$ is
    - (1) the empirical probability of k;
    - (2) the empirical probability of j;
    - (3) the theoretical probability of k;
    - (4) none of the above.

15. Suppose that if k should occur, it will be called a success. If j should occur it will be called a failure. The ratio $\dfrac{k}{k+j}$ is
    - (1) the empirical probability of k;
    - (2) the empirical probability of j;
    - (3) the theoretical probability of k;
    - (4) the theoretical probability of j.

16. Asymptotic means
    - (1) the highest point;
    - (2) the lowest point;
    - (3) approaching a line;
    - (4) not possible.

Chapter 6

17. The advantage of calculating *z scores* is that
      (1) they allow you to know the sample mean;
      (2) they allow you to know the sample standard deviation;
    ● (3) they allow you to compare distributions that come from different populations;
    ✗ (4) none of the above.

18. If you flip a coin a thousand times and plot the results, the distribution will be
      (1) a normal distribution;
      (2) a rectangular distribution;
      (3) a relative distribution;
    ● (4) a binomial distribution.

19. Probability is important in statistics because
    ● (1) it allows us to evaluate the chance that a statistic occurred;
      (2) it allows us to know truth;
      (3) it allows us to make claims based on facts;
      (4) not enough information to answer the question.

20. Suppose a student has a *z score* of –1. That means she
      (1) scored well above the mean;
      (2) had a negative raw score;
    ● (3) scored 1 standard deviation below the mean;
      (4) had the lowest score in the group.

Short-Answer Questions _____

1. Distinguish between theoretical and empirical distributions.

2. Write a paragraph describing the normal curve.

3. Suppose a small college has 500 freshman, 400 sophomores, 300 juniors, and 200 seniors and that you randomly pick one student. What is the probability that the student will be   Total = 1400
      a. a freshman; $\frac{500}{1400} = .36$
      b. a senior;

$\frac{200}{1400} = .14$

52

Chapter 6

c. a sophomore or a junior; $\frac{.400}{1400} + \frac{300}{1400} = .50$

d. not a senior. $\frac{200}{1400} = .14 \quad 1.00 - .14 = .86$

4. Your text has some questions about hobbits, mythical creatures in J. R. R. Tolkien's books. Hobbits have furry feet and love to play games. Suppose some practical joker shaved the feet of the hobbits and reduced their height by one inch. What effect would this have on the mean and standard deviation? Drawing two pictures of the distribution of heights "before" and "after" will help you conceptualize this problem.

5. What is the difference between a binomial distribution and a normal curve?

Problems _____

1. Identify each of the following distributions as theoretical or empirical.
    a. Twelve quarters were tossed in the air 500 times. Each time they landed, the number of heads was recorded.
    b. At Collegiate University, the Registrar recorded the grade point average of every freshman for the years 1975, 1985, 1995, and 2005.
    c. For all Saturdays since the college began, the proportion of rainy days was determined from official weather records.
    d. Each offspring of a single fruit fly was classified as red-eyed or white-eyed.
    e. A normal-shaped distribution was found when 1000 needles from a white pine tree were measured.
    f. When pilots in the Japanese Air Force were weighed, the distribution was positively skewed.

2. Pygmies live in central Africa in a region called Ituri (after the river by that name). Colin Turnbull, who lived with a group of pygmies during the early 1950s, wrote a delightful book called *The Forest People* (1961) telling of his experiences. Turnbull reports that pygmies are less than 4 ½ feet tall. For each of the questions below assume that the height of pygmies is normally distributed with a mean of 4 ft., 3 in. and a standard deviation of 2 inches.
    a. Pygmies live in huts made up of a framework of branches covered with leaves. Materials can be gathered and the hut constructed in an

afternoon. If the opening is 4 feet high, what proportion of the pygmies will have to duck to enter?

b. Suppose only those pygmies who were between 4 ft., 2 in. and 4 ft., 6 in. tall were allowed to sing in a molino ceremony. What proportion would be left out?

c. In the group Turnbull lived with, there was a main group of about 20 families (65 people) plus a subsidiary group of about 4 families (15 people) led by Cephu. If one person from the camp were chosen at random, what is the probability that the person would be from Cephu's subgroup?

3. A classical experiment in extrasensory perception (ESP) consists of asking a participant to tell, without looking, the suit of each card in a deck of Zener cards. There are five suits in the deck so the probability of a chance match between the guess and the card is 1/5 or .20. If only chance is operating, you would expect a participant to get 20 matches in 100 guesses (.20 × 100 = 20). The standard deviation for this mean of 20 is 4.

a. What is the probability of a participant making 23 or more matches in 100 guesses?

b. What is the probability of 27 or more matches in 100 guesses?

c. Suppose a friend of a friend claimed to have ESP and agreed to sit just one time and guess at 100 cards. Suppose she made 36 matches. Calculate the probability of this many, or more, matches if only chance is at work, and carefully write a conclusion.

4. R. B. D'Agnostino (1973) wrote a delightful article about the weight of a 40-pound box of bananas. The problem facing a banana shipper is a rule that a 40-pound box must weigh *at least* 40 pounds upon arrival. Suppose a shipper knows from past experience that, when boxes are packed to have 40 pounds, the standard deviation is four ounces and that on the average a box loses eight ounces in transit.

a. What mean weight should the shipper establish so that only one-fourth of 1% (.0025) of the boxes will arrive with less than 40 pounds?

b. Suppose the shipper adopts the weight you established and ships out 5 million boxes. How many will arrive with less than 40 pounds of bananas?

Chapter 6

5. For the data in Figure 6.1, "Theoretical distribution of 52 draws from a deck of playing cards," the mean is 7.00 and the standard deviation is 3.74. (An ace gets a score of 1, jack = 11, queen = 12, king = 13.) Use the normal curve table to answer the following questions.
   a. What proportion of the distribution would be expected to be aces?
   b. Compare this proportion to that given to Figure 6.1.
   c. Tell why your calculated proportion is less than that given in Figure 6.1 in your text.

6. Women in the U.S. Air Force have hands that are 6.9 inches on the average (from the tip of the middle finger to the heel of the hand). The standard deviation is .34 inches. Assume that hand length is normally distributed.
   a. What proportion have hands longer than 7 inches?
   b. What proportion would have hands shorter than 6 inches?
   c. What proportion would have hands 6.5 to 7.2 inches long?
   d. Of 3000 personnel, how many would have hands longer than 7.5 inches (the mean for male Air Force personnel)?
   e. How long would a woman's hand have to be to put her among the 10% with the longest hands?

7. Psychological and educational tests are often designed so they have a mean of 50 and a standard deviation of 10. The MMPI (Minnesota Multiphasic Personality Inventory) and the Tennessee Self-Concept Scale are examples.
   a. The manual for the MMPI says that scores that are two standard deviations or more above the mean may indicate pathology. Among a thousand persons, how many would be expected to have scores two standard deviations or more above the mean?
   b. What proportion would be expected to score 68 or above?
   c. What proportion would be expected to score between 53 and 63?
   d. What score separates out the lowest one-fifth from the rest?

8. Suppose you live in a state with a lottery system that selects 6 numbers from 36 balls (labeled 1-36) to determine a winner. The order of selection does not influence the outcome. To win, you simply have to match the 6 numbers that the lottery commission selects. What are the odds of you winning that lottery?

CHAPTER 7

Samples, Sampling Distributions
and Confidence Intervals

Summary _____

The fundamental concept discussed in this chapter is the *sampling distribution*, which is a *theoretical* distribution. The standard deviation of any sampling distribution is called the *standard error*; the mean is its *expected value*. A sampling distribution is always of a particular statistic, such as the mean, variance, or correlation coefficient. The sampling distribution of the mean, for example, is a frequency distribution of all possible means (that have the same sample size) from a population. This frequency distribution shows the probability of obtaining any of those sample means with chance draws from the population.

For illustration purposes, you could construct an empirical sampling distribution of the mean. First, choose a population of numbers (you can get a population from the table of random numbers from the back of the book). Second, draw many random samples of the same size. Third, calculate the mean for each sample, and fourth, arrange all the sample means into a frequency polygon. You will find that the polygon looks very much like a normal distribution.

The graph of a sampling distribution of a statistic (either empirical or theoretical) is a picture of the effects that chance has when many random samples of the same size (each with its own statistic) are drawn from a population and for each sample the statistic is calculated. The graph (or table) of these statistics can be used to determine the probability that a particular sample and its statistic came from a particular population.

Sampling distributions come in many shapes (as you will see in later chapters). However, the *sampling distribution of the mean* is a normal distribution if the sample size is large enough.

There are very few phrases or sentences in statistics that are worth memorizing; the Central Limit Theorem (CLT) is probably one of them. The CLT says that as sample size approaches   , the form of the sampling distribution of the mean approaches a normal curve that has a mean, μ, and a standard deviation (standard error), $\dfrac{\sigma}{\sqrt{N}}$. This theorem is true regardless of the form of the population from which the samples are drawn. The CLT only applies to distributions created with sample means.

As can be determined by examining the formula for the standard error of the mean, the sampling distribution of the mean becomes more compact, or narrow, as N is increased.

If the Central Limit Theorem applies, you can use the normal distribution to find the *probability of a sample mean*. When a sample comes from a population with an unknown mean, you can use z scores to determine the probability that the sample mean came from a population with a specific (known) mean. Of course, if the probability is very low, this is reason to believe that the population's unknown mean is different from the specific population mean you used in the z score.

You are justified in using the normal curve to determine probabilities when you know σ and you have an adequate sample. If you cannot meet those requirements (a very common problem in the social sciences), you should use the t distribution. William S. Gosset, known as "Student", developed the t distribution, which is the sampling distribution of $\overline{X}$ when σ must be estimated with   . Each sample size (designated by its particular degrees of freedom) has its own t distribution.

The principal statistic described in this chapter is the *confidence interval*. A confidence interval is an inferential statistical technique that allows you to state, with a specified degree of confidence (such as 95 percent), that an interval of scores (defined by a lower and upper limit) contains the value of an unknown parameter.

For this chapter, the parameter of interest is the mean. Use the t distribution to establish the degree of confidence you select. Thus, the formulas in the chapter give you a *confidence interval about a sample mean*, which tells you about the mean of the population the sample was drawn from.

Chapter 7

Chapter 7 is about how to select samples, and how to use the information you obtain from the sample to understanding something about the population. Using a table of random numbers and the procedures described in the text to select a random sample from the population is the best way to ensure that the sample mirrors the population. In research situations, random samples are usually not feasible, so other methods, such as random assignment and replication are used to establish the validity of the results. Biased samples, in which certain samples of the population are systematically excluded, are to be avoided.

Multiple-Choice Questions _____

1. According to your text, if you draw a random sample, you are assured that
    (1) the sample will always mirror the population;
    (2) you will be somewhat uncertain about the population;
    (3) the conclusions you draw will be correct;
    (4) none of the above.

2. Suppose you had a rectangular distribution (like that of the playing cards, pictured in Chapter 6). Suppose you drew many, many random samples of 25 scores and found the mean. If these means were arranged into a frequency distribution, you would expect the distribution to be
    (1) rectangular;
    (2) bimodal;
    (3) either (1) or (2);
    (4) neither (1) or (2).

3. The Central Limit Theorem (CLT) states that a sampling distribution of the mean approaches the normal curve if
    (1) the population is normally distributed;
    (2) the sample size is large;
    (3) the standard deviation is large;
    (4) any of the above is sufficient.

4. A standard error is a measure of
    (1) central tendency;
    (2) variability;
    (3) correlation;
    (4) none of the above.

Chapter 7

5. Confidence intervals and hypothesis testing are parts of
    (1) descriptive statistics;
    (2) inferential statistics;
    (3) both (1) and (2);
    (4) experimental design.

6. A 95 percent confidence interval means that
    (1) $\overline{X}$ has a 95 percent probability of being in that interval;
    (2) the interval has a 95 percent probability of containing μ;
    (3) either (1) or (2);
    (4) neither (1) or (2).

7. A 95 percent confidence interval of 14 to 17 means that
    (1) 95 percent of the time $\overline{X}$ will be between 14 and 17;
    (2) 95 of the μ's will be between 14 and 17;
    (3) 95 percent of the confidence intervals calculated like this on will contain μ;
    (4) all of the above are correct.

8. Under which of the following conditions is the *t* distribution a normal curve?
    (1) When $df= 1$;
    (2) When the population from which the sample is drawn is normal;
    (3) Both (1) and (2);
    (4) Neither (1) nor (2).

9. A biased sample is one that
    (1) is too small;
    (2) will always lead to a wrong conclusion;
    (3) has certain groups from the population overrepresented or underrepresented;
    (4) is always nonrepresentative.

Chapter 7

10. The names of the mean and standard deviation of a sampling distribution are
    (1) mean, standard deviation;
    (2) mean, standard error;
    (3) expected value, standard deviation;
    (4) expected value, standard error.

11. As N becomes larger, $\sigma_{\bar{x}}$
    (1) becomes smaller;
    (2) becomes larger;
    (3) gets closer in value to the mean;
    (4) gets farther in value from the mean.

12. Uncertainty regarding conclusions about a population can be eliminated by
    (1) drawing a sample;
    (2) drawing a large sample;
    (3) drawing a large, random sample;
    (4) none of the above.

13. The word or phrase closest in meaning to the statistical meaning of the word error is
    (1) arithmetic mistake;
    (2) conceptual mistake;
    (3) deviation;
    (4) statistic.

14. Prof. Gus LaPlace, the mad statistician, was fiddling around in his statistical laboratory one stormy night in 1801. He had a large pile of papers in front of him, each with a measurement written on it. "What would I get," he mused, "if I counted the number of papers I have, took the square root, and then divided that into the standard deviation of all the measurements? Hmmmmmmmmmmmmmmmm...Well, maybe I'll do it tomorrow," he said. If Prof. LaPlace had carried out his plan, he would have discovered (invented)
    (1) the standard error of the standard deviation;
    (2) the standard error of the mean;
    (3) the standard error of the median;
    (4) none of the above.

Chapter 7

15. When the participants who arrive for a study are assigned to a group on the basis of chance
    - (1) random assignment has occurred;
    - (2) random sampling has occurred;
    - (3) the statistical conclusions will be exact;
    - (4) all of the above.

16. The t distribution was invented to handle
    - (1) confidence intervals with more than 99 percent confidence;
    - (2) very large samples;
    - (3) not knowing the values of σ;
    - (4) common arithmetic errors.

17. The difference between a random sample and a biased sample is that
    - (1) biased samples are larger;
    - (2) random samples more accurately reflect the population;
    - (3) biased samples more accurately reflect the population;
    - (4) random samples are larger.

18. As N increases, the mean of the sample is
    - (1) less representative of the population mean;
    - (2) likely to increase in size;
    - (3) likely to decrease in size;
    - (4) more representative of the population mean.

19. A distribution is most likely to be normal when
    - (1) N is large;
    - (2) the population is normal;
    - (3) both (1) and (2);
    - (4) neither (1) nor (2).

Chapter 7

20. A study examining the IQ scores of men at a small private university found that the average IQ for a sample of 5 participants is 140. Which of the following conclusions can be made from this sample?
    - (1) Men from this university are smart;
    - (2) Men from this university are below average IQ;
    - (3) Men from this university are smarter than men from other universities;
    - (4) Not enough information to answer this question.

Short-Answer Questions _____

1. In a sentence, describe the Central Limit Theorem (CLT).

2. Distinguish between the concept of a sampling distribution and the sampling distribution of the mean.

3. Suppose you wanted to know whether the weight of vegetarians was less than that of the general population in the United States. Suppose also that you were fortunate enough to have the weights of a representative sample of 49 male vegetarians who were college age. Now, suppose we know that the average weight of 20-to 29-year-old male Americans is 166 pounds. Suppose further that we also know that weight is *not* normally distributed but is positively skewed. Can you use the techniques described in Chapter 7 to determine the probability that the mean weight of college-age male vegetarians came from a population with a mean weight of 166? Write your conclusion and your reasoning.

4. What improvements could be made to the study described in Question 20 of the multiple choice section to allow for greater confidence concerning the results?

5. What does a confidence interval tell us about a sample mean?

Chapter 7

Problems _____

1. Most companies that manufacture light bulbs advertise their 100-watt bulbs as having a life of 750 hours (Actually, this is an "it depends" statistic. In this case, it depends partly on the number of times the light is turned on and partly on and partly on whether or not the light is ventilated). Let's assume a standard deviation of 100 hours. A consumer organization bought 50 bulbs and burned them until they failed. For the 50 bulbs, the mean number of hours was 725. What is the probability of obtaining a mean this low or lower if the population mean for this brand of bulbs is 750 hours? Write a sentence about advertised claims.

2. Refer to short-answer question 3. Suppose you had the weights of the 49 vegetarians in kilograms. The sum of these weights was 3616 kg. Calculate the mean. What is the probability of obtaining such a mean weight (or one smaller) from a population with a mean of 75.4 kg (166 pounds) and a standard deviation of 10 kg (22 pounds)?

3. Stanley Milgram published a study that became famous because he concluded that average Americans follow orders that lead to apparent injury to others. In Milgram's experiment, a cross-section of Americans increased the apparent shock they were administering to a fellow participant to an average of 285 volts. Suppose a psychologist at a small, New England college with humanitarian ideals was sure that students at her college would not be so cruel. She set up the same apparatus and procedures and gathered data on a random sample of 36 students from her school. She found

$$\Sigma X = 11,340 \qquad\qquad \Sigma X^2 = 3,698,100$$

Construct a 99 percent confidence interval about the mean. Interpret this confidence interval by describing students at the small college.

4. A teacher was interested in the mathematical ability of graduating high school seniors in her state. She gave a 32-item test to a random sample of 75 seniors with the following results: $\Sigma X = 1275$, $\Sigma X = 23, 525$. Establish a 95% confidence interval about the sample mean, and write a sentence that explains the interval you found.

Chapter 7

5. The instructor of a popular course on health used a number of films in her course. After a film, each student filled out a questionnaire. High scores indicated that the film was valuable. Over the previous five years, the scores were negatively skewed with a mean of 33 and a standard deviation of 2.40. This year the instructor showed students a new film on smoking, and got the following statistics: $\Sigma X = 1224$, $\Sigma X^2 = 41818$. Calculate a 95% confidence interval about the sample mean and tell what the students thought of the film.

6. In the field of testing it is common to design a test so that the population mean is 50. The California Personality Inventory (CPI), which is designed to access the general population, has these characteristics. One of the scales of the CPI assesses socialization. Suppose that a researcher thought that fraternity and sorority members are more sociable than the general population. She gathered data on 49 Greeks, finding a mean of 52 and a standard deviation of 10. Find the 99% confidence interval about the mean. Do the data indicate that Greeks are more sociable than average?

7. Draw a random sample with $N = 6$ from the following scores. Write down each step in your procedure.

21   31   17   13   02   09   57   26   72   140

8. From that sample in Question 7, what is the standard error of the mean? Write a sentence explaining what standard error of the mean reveals about the population mean.

CHAPTER 8

Hypothesis Testing and Effect Size:
One-Sample Designs

Summary_____

This chapter is the first of a two-chapter sequence that covers the basics of *null hypothesis statistical testing (NHST)*. NHST is a statistical tool that helps you make decisions about populations when you have sample data. This chapter introduces you to techniques that are appropriate when data are gathered from only *one sample*. Techniques that apply data from two or more samples are covered in later chapters.

There are several steps involved in NHST:
1. Hypothesize that the sample's statistic (for example, $\overline{X}$ or r) came from a particular population with a parameter (μ_0 or ρ). This is a hypothesis of equality and is called the null hypothesis (H_0).
2. Choose a sampling distribution that shows the probability of different sample statistics when samples are drawn from the population that has the particular parameter. In this chapter, the proper sampling distribution is the *t distribution*.
3. Using the proper sampling distribution, determine the probability of your sample mean, or one more extreme. This probability is correct, *if the null hypothesis is true*.
4. If the probability is small (equal to or less than .05), conclude that the null hypothesis is incorrect and that your sample data have likely come from some other population.
5. If the probability is large (greater than .05), conclude that the data are consistent with the null hypothesis and perhaps with other hypotheses as well. In statistical terms, you are now left with insufficient evidence to reject the null hypothesis.

Expanding on steps 4 and 5, the continuum of probability is divided into two regions. The *rejection region* is characterized by small probabilities and the decision to *reject the null hypothesis*. The other region is characterized by larger probabilities and the decision to *retain the null hypothesis,* which is also referred to as *failure to*

Chapter 8

reject the null hypothesis. The dividing point on the continuum is α (alpha). The experimenter chooses the α level, which is sometimes referred to as the *level of significance.* Alpha is typically .05 or less.

For the two statistics in this chapter, $\overline{X}$ and r, the t distribution is the proper sampling distribution. A t test on one sample gives a t value. This t value is evaluated by comparing it to the values shown in the t *distribution* table, which shows selected t values called *critical values.* These critical values are those points on the distribution that correspond to commonly chosen α levels. To find the appropriate critical value in the t distribution table, you must know the *degrees of freedom* appropriate for the data. In testing a sample mean, $df = N\text{-}1$, where N is the number of scores. In testing a correlation coefficient, $df = N\text{-}2$, where N is the number of pairs of score. In later chapters that explain other designs, there are other formulas for df.

If the data-based t value is greater than the critical value associated with α in the table, *reject the null hypothesis.* If the data-based t value is less than the critical value, *retain the null hypothesis.* Results that lead to a rejected null hypothesis are said to be *statistically significant.* Not having sufficient evidence to reject of the null hypothesis does not mean that the experiment is a failure. There are several reasons that a test may fail to reject the null hypothesis.

In addition to the null hypothesis, NHST requires an alternative hypothesis (H_1). The most common alternative hypothesis is *two-tailed*, an alternative that places half the rejection region in each tail of the sampling distribution. A two-tailed test permits the rejection of the null hypothesis for means that are either larger or smaller than the null hypothesis mean and for correlation coefficients that are either positive or negative. One kind of one-tailed test permits rejection of the null hypothesis only if the sample mean is larger than the null hypothesis mean. Such a test cannot detect a sample mean that is smaller, no matter how small.

Like all decision-making aids, NHST can lead to wrong conclusions. If the null hypothesis is indeed true, and the data lead you to reject it, you have made a *Type I error.* The probability of a Type I error is never greater than α, which is set by the researcher.

Chapter 8

If the null hypothesis is actually false and the data lead you to retain it, you have made a *Type II error*. The probability of a Type II error is symbolized by β. Among the several factors that determine β are (1) α – the smaller α is, the larger β is, and vice versa, and (2) the actual difference between the population sampled from and the null hypothesis population – the larger the difference, the smaller β is.

The formula for the *effect size index, d,* tells you about the size of the difference between the mean of the population that the sample was drawn from and the mean of the null hypothesis population. *d* values of 0.20, 0.50, and 0.80 characterize small, medium and large effect sizes for a one-sample *t* test. An effect size estimate is an increasingly popular way to describe differences.

Multiple-Choice Questions _____

1. In NHST, the hypothesis that is tested is about a
    - (1) sample;
    - (2) population;
    - (3) both (1) and (2);
    - (4) neither (1) nor (2).

2. Using NHST, you can conclude that the null hypothesis is
    - (1) probably true;
    - (2) probably false;
    - (3) both (1) and (2) are possible conclusions;
    - (4) neither (1) nor (2) are possible conclusions.

3. The *t* distribution, as a sampling distribution, gives the probability of events when
    - (1) the null hypothesis is true;
    - (2) the null hypothesis is false;
    - (3) both (1) and (2) are correct at times;
    - (4) the alternative hypothesis is not identified.

Chapter 8

4. Suppose the difference between a sample mean and the null hypothesis mean was in the rejection region of the sampling distribution. This means that the difference is
    (1) probably the result of mistakes;
    (2) unreasonable; it is either too large or too small;
    (3) probably due to chance;
    (4) probably not due to chance.

5. Which phrase goes with "in the rejection region"?
    (1) calculated probability is small;
    (2) reject the null hypothesis;
    (3) both (1) and (2);
    (4) neither (1) nor (2).

6. When an experimenter uses $\alpha = .05$, the rejection region is _____
    (1) 95 percent of the curve;
    (2) 5 percent of the curve;
    (3) 5 percent of a one-tailed test and 10 percent of a two-tailed test;
    (4) 10 percent of a one-tailed test and 5 percent of a two-tailed test.

7. When we reject the null hypothesis, we have evidence that the difference observed is
    (1) due to chance;
    (2) very small;
    (3) unlikely to be due to chance;
    (4) a Type I error.

8. An effect size index is most closely associated with which phrase below?
    (1) The α level chosen by the researcher;
    (2) The probability of a Type II error;
    (3) The size of the difference between the sample mean and the null hypothesis mean;
    (4) The size of the rejection region.

Chapter 8

9. Suppose you obtained a sample from a population for which the null hypothesis was true. On the basis of a *t* test, you failed to reject the null hypothesis. You have made a
    (1) Type I error;
    (2) Type II error;
    (3) correct decision;
    (4) any of the above; more information is needed.

10. Suppose you obtained a sample from a population different from the one specified by the null hypothesis. On the basis of a *t* test, you failed to reject the null hypothesis. You have made a
    (1) Type I error;
    (2) Type II error;
    (3) correct decision;
    (4) any of the above; more information is needed.

11. "$p > .05$" means that
    (1) the null hypothesis should be rejected;
    (2) the difference between the statistic and the null hypothesis parameter is statistically significant;
    (3) both (1) and (2);
    (4) neither (1) nor (2).

12. We reject the null hypothesis when
    (1) $p > .05$;
    (2) $p < .05$;
    (3) not enough information to answer this question.

13. Which of the following shows a correct match-up of an alternative hypothesis and its one- or two-tailed test?
    (1) $H_1: \mu_0 = \mu_1$; one-tailed;
    (2) $H_1: \mu_0 < \mu_1$; two-tailed;
    (3) both (1) and (2);
    (4) neither (1) nor (2).

Chapter 8

14. The choice of an alternative hypothesis has an effect on
    - (1) conclusions you may draw;
    - (2) α level;
    - (3) which null hypothesis you are testing;
    - (4) all of the above.

15. Which answer below belongs with the concept of a two-tailed test of significance?
    - (1) $H_1: \mu_1 > \mu_0$;
    - (2) Type II error;
    - (3) both (1) and (2);
    - (4) a divided rejection region.

16. A one-tailed test is proper when
    - (1) you do not have enough data for a two-tailed test;
    - (2) you have only one sample, not two;
    - (3) you are interested in finding out only that the effect of a treatment is to increase the scores;
    - (4) you want to make the standard error of the mean as small as possible.

17. When the *t* distribution is used to determine the significance of a correlation coefficient, the null hypothesis is that the population correlation coefficient is
    - (1) –1.00;
    - (2) 0.00;
    - (3) 1.00;
    - (4) the coefficient obtained from the sample.

18. Your text concluded that the Frito-Lay corporation, which claims to put 269.3 grams of Doritos tortilla chips in their packages, actually puts in _____ that amount.
    - (1) about;
    - (2) exactly;
    - (3) significantly more than;
    - (4) significantly less than.

Chapter 8

19. The custom of using an α level of .05 got its start in the field of
    (1) astronomy;
    (2) agriculture;
    (3) physics;
    (4) government.

20. If the t test value is less than the critical value on the table, _____ the null
    hypothesis even though you could be making a _____ error.
    (1) reject, Type I;
    (2) retain, Type II;
    (3) reject, Type II;
    (4) retain, Type I.

Short-Answer Questions _____

1. Distinguish between Type I and Type II errors.

2. Distinguish between $\alpha = .05$ and $p = .05$.

3. Distinguish between rejecting and retaining the null hypothesis.

4. Write an interpretation of each of the following situations.
   a. Sometimes natural events produce experiences that cannot be
      duplicated in the laboratory. The abduction, confinement, and release
      of hostages is an example. Does this experience have any effect on the
      personality characteristic of dominance? The California Personality
      Inventory has a scale for Dominance (D_o); high scores indicate
      confidence, assertiveness, and task orientation, and low scores
      indicate an unassuming and unforceful person. A score of 50 is the
      mean for the D_o scale; the standard deviation is 10. Suppose that the
      mean D_o score for a group of 8 released hostages was 42. A t test
      produced a value of 2.25. The calculated value of d was 0.80. Write
      the null hypothesis and a conclusion about the effects of confinement.
   b. Are teachers accurate at assessing the honesty of their students? Is
      there any relationship between teacher ratings and test scores on a test
      of honesty? This last question can be answered with a correlation
      coefficient. Murphy and Davidshofer (1991, p. 121) report a Pearson r

Chapter 8

of .62 between teacher ratings of honesty and a test designed to assess honesty. If the data were based on 15 students, what conclusion can you draw?

5. Write an interpretation of each of the following situations.
   a. Stanley Milgram found in the early 1960s that a cross section of Americans was willing to administer an average of 285 volts to other participants in an experiment (Milgram, 1963). Have times changed? Suppose that the study was replicated today with 20 participants who were willing to administer an average of only 240 volts. A *t* test produced a value of 2.00. Write the null hypothesis and a conclusion about the difference between today and the early 1960s in people's willingness to administer shock to others.
   b. Matsumoto, Kasri, and Kooken (1999) found that there was a strong correlation between people of different cultures and facial expressions. That is, there was strong agreement of what a facial expression represented across cultures. If the correlation was .44, and was based on a sample of 25, what conclusion would be appropriate?

6. Write a paragraph or two explaining NHST.

Problems _____

1. Remember the Personal Control Scores in Chapter 2? The mean PC score for all college students is 51. What about students who are in academic difficulty? How do they feel about the control of their personal lives? The hypothetical data in this problem are PC scores for students in academic difficulty. Perform a *t* test, calculate an effect size index, and write a conclusion about feelings of personal control among students in academic difficulty.

48 44 53 35 58 42 55 37 50 46 40 32

Chapter 8

2. Every year thousands of college-bound American high school seniors take the Scholastic Aptitude Test (SAT). During one recent year the mean score was 896 (math plus verbal). Summary statistics for one small high school follow. How do the students compare to the national norm? State the null hypothesis, choose an alternative hypothesis, perform a t test, calculate the effect size index, and write a conclusion.

$$\Sigma X = 24,206 \qquad \Sigma X^2 = 22,716,411$$
$$N = 26$$

3. Miller (1956), in a classic study, demonstrated that participants can store 7 bits of information in short term memory. Assume you believe you can train students to do better by having them memorize 10 digit phone numbers. You train your participants for 10 days, test them and obtain the information below. Analyze the data with a t test and an effect size index. Write an interpretation.

$$\Sigma X = 235 \qquad \Sigma X^2 = 1931$$
$$N = 30$$

Raw Scores:

9	5	8	7	9	8	6	6	7	5
8	6	9	8	7	11	10	8	6	9
11	8	8	9	6	9	6	7	7	12

4. The Rathus Assertiveness Schedule is a 30-item questionnaire; the mean score for men is 11. Suppose that the student development office at your college conducted a 6-week assertiveness course. At the end of the course, the male participants had the following scores. Perform a t test, calculate the effect size index, and write a conclusion about the assertiveness course.

25	36	-1	28	24	53	-3	46	26

Chapter 8

5. As you may recall from problem 30 in the textbook, when people choose a number between 1 and 10, the mean is 6. To investigate the effects of blatant, direct stimuli on behavior, a researcher embedded many low numbers (1 to 3) in a video clip. Each one was very obvious. Afterward the participants were asked to "choose a number between 1 and 10." Analyze the data with a t test and an effect size index. Write an interpretation of these data. In addition, using your analysis of Problem 30, write an interpretation based on both data sets.

$$\Sigma X = 200 \qquad \qquad \Sigma X^2 = 1206$$
$$N = 40$$

Raw Scores:

5	1	3	2	3	3	4	4	7	5
7	6	6	7	3	8	4	9	5	6	4
3	6	1	2	8	7	5	4	7	6	3
7	8	2	8	1	9	7	4			

CHAPTER 9

Hypothesis Testing, Effect Size and
Confidence Intervals: Two-Sample Designs

Summary _____

For the simplest *experiment*, two populations are identified. The two populations might be reaction times after drinking coffee or decaf, test anxiety scores during the semester versus during finals week, or percent of recall after being awake or asleep. The question is whether the mean of one population, μ_1, is different from the mean of a second population, μ_2.

The two different populations are the two levels of the *independent variable*. A sample from each population is measured on the *dependent variable* and sample means are calculated. The means of the two samples will probably be different. Null hypothesis statistical testing (NHST) may permit you to decide the reason for the difference.

The *logic of null hypothesis statistical testing (NHST)* is to tentatively hypothesize that $\mu_1 = \mu_2$. This hypothesis is the null hypothesis and is symbolized H_0. If H_0 is true, then the difference in the two sample means is due to sampling fluctuation. A sampling distribution such as the *t* distribution shows the probability of differences between sample means *if H_0 is true*. By finding the probability of the observed difference in sample means, the researcher can draw a conclusion. If the probability is small (.05 or less, for example), H_0 can be rejected. (because such sample data are unlikely if H_0 is true). If the probability is larger (.051 or larger, for example), retain H_0. A *t* test gives you the probability of the observed data *if H_0 is true*.

The probability value that separates rejecting H_0 from retaining H_0 is called α. .05 is the largest commonly accepted α value. The α value is also referred to as the significance level. If the probability of the observed difference is less than α, the difference is *statistically significant*. Note that this logic is *identical* to the logic in the previous chapter. The difference is in the comparison. In this chapter, we compare *two sample means*. In Chapter 8, we compared the *mean of a sample to the mean of a population*.

Chapter 9

The last step in data analysis is a carefully worded statement about the effects of the independent variable on the dependent variable. Terms that describe the variables are used in this statement, not generic terms such as experimental group and dependent variable. Once the statistics are completed, write a clear explanation of what the data show.

In addition to deciding on an α level before the data are gathered, a researcher must also decide whether the t test will be one or two-tailed. *Two-tailed tests*, which are much more common, allow a conclusion that μ_1 is larger OR that it is smaller than μ_2. A *one-tailed test* places the entire rejection region in one tail of the sampling distribution; thus, if the relationship of the sample means is opposite that expected by the researcher, the null hypothesis cannot be rejected, no matter how different the means are.

Paired-samples designs are two-group experiments in which the scores consist of pairs. The pairs might exist before the experiment begins (*natural pairs*); one member of the pair serves in the experimental group and the other in the control group. Pairs might be formed by matching the participants on some variable related to the dependent variable (*matched pairs*). Finally, participants might serve in a before-and-after design (*repeated measures*) which is the most common paired-samples design. The t distribution for a paired-samples design has N-1 degrees of freedom (where N is the number of pairs).

An independent-samples design occurs when the scores are not paired in any logical way. The t distribution for an independent-samples design has $N_1+N_2 -2$ degrees of freedom.

The t distribution gives you accurate probabilities when certain conditions are met. For the independent-samples t test, the two conditions are:
1. the populations are normally distributed, and
2. the populations have variances that are equal,

In addition to accurate probabilities, correct conclusions depend on control of extraneous variables. The most common way to control the extraneous variables is to randomly assign participants to levels of the independent variable.

Chapter 9

Besides testing a null hypothesis about a difference between two levels of the independent variable, you can calculate a *confidence interval* about the mean difference. A confidence interval consists of a lower and upper limit and is for a specified degree of confidence, such as 90, 95, or 99 percent. The two limits capture a range of values. Within this range, you can expect, with a certain degree of confidence, to find the difference that exists between the two population means that the two samples are drawn from.

This chapter provides additional information about *effect size*. The *effect size index, d*, describes the size of the difference between the two populations. Although the formulas for *d* differ somewhat for independent-sample designs and paired-sample designs, values of 0.20, 0.50, and 0.80 indicate small, medium and large effects, respectively for both designs.

The more powerful a statistical test is, the better its ability to detect a false null hypothesis. Power is equal to 1-β, where β is the probability of a Type II error. (For an excellent article on power, see Cohen [1992]). The factors that determine power are:
1. the actual effect size (or difference between populations)
2. the size of the standard error of a difference, which is governed by N and sample variability, and
3. alpha (α).

Multiple-Choice Questions _____

1. For a simple experiment, which of the following is true?
   (1) for the null hypothesis, assume that the two groups represent different populations;
   (2) apply the dependent variable to both groups and then measure the changes in the independent variable;
   (3) find the probability that the two samples are from different populations by using a *t* distribution;
   (4) treat both groups exactly alike except for one thing.

Chapter 9

2. The logic of hypothesis testing is to assume that two populations have
    (1) means that are equal and then see if sample data will permit you to conclude that they are probably equal;
    (2) means that are equal and then see if sample data will permit you to conclude that they are probably unequal;
    (3) means that are not equal and then see if sample data will permit you to conclude that they are probably unequal;
    (4) means that are not equal and then see if sample data will permit you to conclude that they are probably equal.

3. Which conclusion is *not* appropriate when using hypothesis testing?
    (1) The two sample means probably came from two different populations.
    (2) The two samples probably came from the same population.
    (3) Retain the hypothesis that the two sample means came from the same population.
    (4) All of the above.

4. In an independent-samples design, the null hypothesis is that
    (1) the population mean of one group is equal to that of a second group;
    (2) the population mean of one group is larger to smaller than that of a second group;
    (3) the sample mean of one group is equal to that of a second group;
    (4) the sample mean of one group is larger or smaller than that of a second group.

5. According to your text the reason we do experiments is to be able to tell
    (1) whether all extraneous variables were controlled;
    (2) whether the samples were representative of the population;
    (3) how dependent variable scores are affected by the independent variable;
    (4) all of the above.

Chapter 9

6. " _____ depends on the number of observations minus the number of relations among the observations" is a statement about how to calculate
   (1) df;
   (2) the difference between population means;
   (3) $s_{\bar{x}}$;
   (4) none of the above.

7. An experimenter found one sample mean of 13 based on an N of 8. The second sample mean was 18 based on an N of 6. The design
   (1) was a paired-samples one;
   (2) was an independent-samples one;
   (3) could be either a paired- or an independent-samples one.

8. A one-tailed test of significance produced a t equal to –2.30, significant at the .05 level. The design of this experiment
   (1) was a paired-samples design;
   (2) was an independent-samples design;
   (3) could have been either a paired- or independent-samples design.

9. With an acknowledgment to Sesame Street, "Which of these things is not like the others, which of these things doesn't belong?"
   (1) repeated measures;
   (2) natural pairs;
   (3) independent samples;
   (4) matched pairs.

Chapter 9

10. There has been bad blood between the Montague family and the Capulet family for a good while. In this modern day, resolution can be achieved by using a psychological test. In the test of "propensity to fall in love," the mean of the 6 Montagues was 54 and the mean of the 10 Capulets was 64. (Italian norms show a national average of 100.) When a statistician compared the families with a *t* test, a value of 2.13 was obtained. If you adopt an α level of .05 (two-tailed test), you should conclude that the Capulets are

    (1) significantly more loving than the Montagues;
    (2) significantly less loving than the Montagues;
    (3) not significantly different from the Montagues;
    (4) not yet comparable; additional information is needed.

11. In an independent samples design the Hatfields had a mean score of 25; the mean score of the McCoys was 26. Low scores mean better performance. The researcher ran a two-tailed test with α at .05. A *t* value of 1.99 was found. Which of the following is true?

    (1) If $df = 40$, the Hatfields are significantly better than the McCoys;
    (2) If $df = 40$, the McCoys are significantly better than the Hatfields;
    (3) If $df = 120$, the Hatfields and the McCoys are not significantly different;
    (4) If $df = 120$, the Hatfields are significantly better than the McCoys;
    (5) If $df = 12$, the McCoys are significantly better than the Hatfields.

12. Which of the following variables affect the size of the standard error of a difference?

    (1) difference between sample means;
    (2) sample size;
    (3) both (1) and (2);
    (4) neither (1) nor (2).

13. $p < .05$ means that the difference between sample means

    (1) fell outside the rejection region;
    (2) should be attributed to chance rather than to the independent variable;
    (3) should be declared "not significant";
    (4) none of the above.

Chapter 9

14. Which of the following answers has effect size indexes that are considered small?
>   (1) 0.01 and 0.05;
>   (2) 0.10 and 0.20;
>   (3) both (1) and (2);
>   (4) neither (1) nor (2).

15. The power of a statistical test is defined as
>   (1) α;
>   (2) β;
>   (3) $1 - α$;
>   (4) $1 - β$.

16. The 95 percent confidence interval about a mean difference was –3.0 minutes to 6.5 minutes. The null hypothesis that the two population means are equal
>   (1) can be rejected at the .05 level;
>   (2) can be rejected at the .01 level;
>   (3) can be rejected at both the .05 and the .01 level;
>   (4) should be retained.

17. The *main* difference between a paired-sample and independent-sample *t* is
>   (1) sample size;
>   (2) *df*;
>   (3) the organization of the data;
>   (4) the analysis of the data.

18. For a normally distributed set of scores, if is often *best* to use the design that has the most power. Which of the following designs has the most power?
>   (1) paired-sample;
>   (2) independent sample;
>   (3) neither.

19. Which of the following has an influence on the *power* of a statistical test?
>   (1) sample size;
>   (2) alpha;
>   (3) actual difference;
>   (4) all of the above.

Chapter 9

20. The *df* are most closely related to
      (1) sample size;
      (2) alpha;
      (3) actual difference between population means;
      (4) choice of a one- or two-tailed test.

Short-Answer Questions _____

1. Identify the design and the degrees of freedom for each of the following experiments.
   a. To determine which is the lowest form of humor, 14 sophomores rated a pun and then a limerick for lowness.
   b. To determine which is the lowest humor, a Greek physician found the amount of blood and the amount of lymph in the sole of each of 21 Greek philosophers.
   c. To determine which is the longest form of humerus, an anthropologist measured that bone in 15 men and 15 women and compared the sexes.
   d. To determine whether the psychologist or the philosopher had the lowest form of humus in his garden, 12 samples were taken from the garden of each. The amount of humus was determined for each sample.
   e. Every student knows, of course, that the very lowest form of humor is test humor. To determine if test humor has become even lower over time, the tests of 34 young professors were compared for lowness to the tests of each of their own teachers when they were young.

2. Identify the design and the degrees of freedom for each of the following experiments.
   a. The effect of cola on attention was measured by counting the number of "eye reversals" in videotapes of students reading the *Iliad*. Fifty participants were observed for 10 minutes. Each consumed 12 oz. of cola during 5 minutes. The 50 were then observed for 10 more minutes.
   b. 21 famous sociologists rate their attitude toward statistics and then identified their best student who had obtained a PhD in sociology. Attitudes toward statistics were then obtained from these 21 also.

   c. A consumer group compared two detergents, Bold and Tide, to determine which was better. 24 white wash cloths that had been soaked in mud for 10 hours were washed (12 cloths for each brand). Afterward the amount of light reflected from each cloth was measured with a photometer.

   d. The mean IQ, reading level, and age of a classroom of 25 Native Americans was equal to that of a classroom of 25 Hispanic Americans. For each student, attitude toward school was measured and mean attitudes compared.

   e. Eight cancer patients rated their emotionality while sitting in a large blue waiting room. Later they rated their emotionality while sitting in a small yellow waiting room.

3. List the factors that influence whether or not you reject the null hypothesis. Explain how each factor influences the final decision.

4. A two-group experiment might have the phrase "$p = .01$." Explain by finishing the sentence: The probability is .01 that...

5. Please list and explain the three factors your text identified that influence whether or not you reach correct conclusions when you use a t test.

6. Those interested in the nature of *Homo sapiens* have often asked, "Is experience necessary for this behavior, or will it develop without any experience?" One way of answering this question has been to study different cultures. The rationale is that, if the cultures are quite different but the behavior is the same, then experience is not necessary. In the case of walking, a behavior of fundamental importance, comparisons have been made between Native American cultures and Anglo American cultures. Some Native American babies spent most of the day bound to a board on their mothers' backs and had few opportunities to creep, crawl, and kick. The age (in months) at which children from the two cultures first walked was the dependent variable in this study.

     A dozen Native American children began to walk at a mean age of 12.3 months; for a dozen Anglo American children, the mean was 12.1 months. A t test on the means produced a value of 0.05. Identify the design as

Chapter 9

independent samples or correlated samples, give the critical value for *t* at the .05 level, and write a conclusion about the effect of experience on walking behavior.

7. This is an experiment on set (previous experience) that is from the same tradition as the "two-string problem" in your text. This experiment is based on one by Luchins (1942) and is referred to as the "water-jar problem." Participants mentally used three jars to measure out a specific amount of water. For example, if the three jars held 12.4, and 3 units and the task was to obtain 5 units, you could fill the 12-unit jar and from it fill the 4- and 3-unit jars once, leaving 5 units in the larger jar. After giving the kind of explanation you have just received, Luchins gave participants the series of eight problems below. It will be worthwhile to work these problems in order yourself, noting in the margin the number of seconds it takes you to solve each problem. Work the eight problems before reading on.

Problem	Jars Contain			Obtain
1	21	127	3	100
2	14	163	25	99
3	18	43	10	5
4	9	42	6	21
5	20	59	4	31
6	23	49	3	20
7	15	39	3	18
8	28	76	3	25

Some participants worked the problems in the order that you followed, and some started with Problem No. 8. The dependent variable was the time necessary to solve Problem No. 8. The independent variable was whether the participant had received the "set" generated by working Problems 1 through 7. (If you worked the problems as suggested, you established such a set.)

Those who worked Problem No. 8 first required significantly less time to find an answer than those who worked the problem last. Identify the design as independent- or repeated-samples, and write a conclusion about this experiment on set.

Chapter 9

8. Explain what a powerful statistical test is. How can power of a statistical test be increased?

9. What is the best type of statistic to use if you are comparing a pre-test post-test experiment?

10. List two reasons to run a paired-sample t when it is possible.

Problems _____

1. In an early study of the effects of frustration on feelings of hostility, Miller and Bugelski (1948) had a group of boys at a camp rate their attitudes toward two minority groups (Mexicans and Japanese). The campers then participated in a long, difficult testing session that kept them away from their weekly movie. Finally the boys again rated their attitudes toward the minority groups. The scores below are similar to those of Miller and Bugelski; they represent the number of unfavorable traits attributed to minorities. Analyze them with a t test and an effect size index, and explain your analysis.

Participant	Before Testing $\overset{X}{}$	After Testing $\overset{Y}{}$	$\underline{D}$	$\underline{D^2}$
1	5	6	-1	1
2	4	4	0	0
3	3	5	-2	4
4	3	4	-1	1
5	2	4	-2	4
6	2	3	-1	1
7	1	3	-2	4
8	0	2	-2	4

$N=8$

$\Sigma X = 20$ $\Sigma Y = 31$

$\overline{X} = 2.5$ $\overline{Y} = 3.875$ $\Sigma D = -11$ $\Sigma D^2 = 19$

2. R. S. Lazarus (1964) had two groups of participants watch a film that showed accidents occurring in a workshop. The accidents were gruesome events such as fingers being cut off and a plank being thrown through a man's midsection by a circular saw. One group was instructed to remain detached from the events. The other group was instructed to become involved. Heart rate was monitored and increases noted. The data that follow are similar to those obtained by Lazarus. Analyze the data with a t test and an effect size index

and comment on human ability to control emotions (as measured by heart rate increase).

Detached	Involved
23	31
21	27
19	24
15	23
14	21
12	14
10	

3. As a result of research before 1900, E. L. Thorndike concluded that animals were incapable of learning by imitation. In 1901, however, L. L. Hobhouse reported that cats, dogs, otters, elephants, monkeys, and chimpanzees could learn by imitation. Suppose the following study was conducted to study the question. One group of hungry cats was shown food being obtained from under a vase. Another group was not, although there was food under the vase. Shortly afterward, the time (in seconds) required to upset the vase and find the food was recorded for each animal. Results are given below. Calculate a 95% confidence interval. Which of the two theorists does your analysis support?

Shown	Not Shown
18	25
15	22
15	21
12	19
11	16
9	15

4. A number of studies have used animals to examine the relationship between neuroticism and alcoholism. Here is a typical study. From each of seven litters two cats were randomly selected and assigned to one of two groups. One group was subjected to a procedure that induced

temporary neurosis. Then all cats were offered milk spiked with 5% alcohol. The amount consumed in three minutes was measured in milliliters. Decide if this is a correlated-samples design or an independent-samples design. Analyze the data with a 99% confidence interval. Comment on the relationship between neuroticism and alcohol consumption.

Littermates	No Experimental Neurosis	Experimental Neurosis
1	63	88
2	59	90
3	52	74
4	51	78
5	46	78
6	44	61
7	38	54

5. A 1984 study by Benjamin, Cavell, and Shallenberger tested the question of whether a student should change an answer on a multiple choice question when re-checking a test. They found that changing answers on multiple-choice exams *increased* scores on exams. Assume they found the following data.

Scores on exams for students who changed answers		Scores on exams for students who stuck with initial response	
85	7225	74	5476
73	5329	75	5625
69	4761	88	7744
99	9801	70	4900
87	7569	71	5041

$N=5$

$\bar{X}=82.6$ $\quad \Sigma X = 413 \quad \Sigma X^2 = 34685$

$\bar{X}=75.6$ $\quad \Sigma X = 378 \quad \Sigma X^2 = 28786$

What is the appropriate statistical test for this experiment? Analyze the data and write a conclusion.

CHAPTER 10

Analysis of Variance: One-Way Classification

Summary _____

Analysis of variance (ANOVA) is another NHST technique that allows you to draw conclusions about populations from sample data. The null hypothesis of a one-way ANOVA is that the means of the populations that the two or more samples come from are equal. If the data allow you to reject this null hypothesis, you can tell a story about the effects of the various levels of the independent variable on the dependent variable.

The *rationale of ANOVA* is important. To really grasp the rationale, you must have clear ideas of how the *two estimates of the population variance* are found. Here is the rationale of ANOVA presented in two different ways, first in list form and then with paragraphs and pictures.

Rationale of ANOVA---I

A.   Assume that the variances of the populations from which the samples were taken are equal. Estimate this variance by calculating a variance for each sample and averaging them. Put this estimate of the population variance aside for now.

B.   When the null hypothesis is true:

1.   When the null hypothesis is true, the sample means will not vary much from each other. The variability among the means can be measured with a variance of the means. Calculate this variance and multiply it by a factor that makes it equal to the population variance that was estimated previously (in A above).

2.   Construct a ratio. Put the variance that measures the variability among sample means in the numerator and the variance that measures the population variance in the denominator. Expect that this ratio (called F) will be about 1.00, although some variability in the ratio is expected because of sampling variation. The variation of this F ratio is a sampling distribution of F. F values with probabilities of .05 and .01 are in the table in your text.

Chapter 10

C. When the null hypothesis is false:
    1. When the null hypothesis is *false*, the sample means will be different from one another. This variability can be measured with a variance, producing a value that will be larger than the one you get when the samples come from the same population.
    2. Construct a ratio. Put the variance produced by sample means drawn from different populations in the numerator and the variance that measures population variance in the denominator. Expect that the ratio will be larger than 1.00.
D. Using data from an experiment, calculate the F value. The probability of this F value when the null hypothesis is true is given in Table F in your text. If this probability is low (.05 or less), reject the null hypothesis. If the probability is not low (.051 or greater), retain the null hypothesis.

Rationale of ANOVA---II

When the Null Hypothesis is True: Look at Population A in Figure 10.1. Suppose you drew three samples from Population A. For each sample, a variance, ^{2} can be calculated. Each ^{2} is an estimate of σ^2, the population variance. Pooling the three sample variances provides an even better estimate of σ^2.

Population A

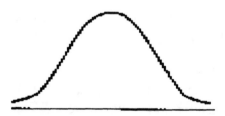

Figure 10.1 Population A with variance, a^2. Used to illustrate ANOVA when the null hypothesis is true

The three samples also yield three $\overline{X}$'s. The three means, which will be fairly close together, provide another way to estimate σ^2. The sample means, N, and algebra produce another accurate estimate of σ^2.

Chapter 10

Finally, if the second estimate of σ^2 is divided by the first estimate of σ^2, a ratio (the F ratio) will be about 1.00. This is the result when the null hypothesis is true, which is the case when all the samples are drawn from Population A.

When the Null Hypothesis is False: Look at Figure 10.2, which shows three populations, B, C, and D, whose variances are equal. Suppose you drew a sample from each population. For each sample, a variance, s^2, can be calculated. Each s^2 is an estimate of the variance, σ^2, the variance that is the same for all three populations.

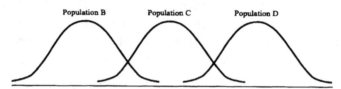

Population B   Population C   Population D

Figure 10.2   Populations B, C, and D, which have variances that are equal but means that are different. Used to illustrate ANOVA when the null hypothesis is false.

The three samples also yield three $\overline{X}$'s, which again can be used to estimate σ^2. This time, however, the means will not be close together. Now, the estimate of σ^2 that is based on sample means will not be accurate; it will *overestimate* the actual size of σ^2.

Finally, if the second estimate of σ^2 (based on sample means) is divided by the first estimate of σ^2 (based on averaging $\hat{s}^2$), the ratio will be greater than 1.00. This is the result when the null hypothesis is false (the three samples are from different populations).

Thus, if the ratio of the two variances is much greater than 1.00, there is evidence that the null hypothesis is false. How big is "much greater?" The F distribution shows F values that occur 5% and 1% of the time when the null hypothesis is true. If your experiment produces a calculated F value that is larger than the tabled F value, reject the null hypothesis and conclude that the samples did not all come from the same population.

The degrees of freedom for the numerator of the F ratio is $K-1$, where K is the number of groups. The *df* for the denominator is $N_{tot} - K$.

Chapter 10

Tests Subsequent to ANOVA

If the data allow you to reject the null hypothesis, further tests are informative. These tests are either *a priori* or *post hoc* tests. *A priori* tests require that a limited number of comparisons be chosen on logical grounds prior to data analysis. *Post hoc* tests allow you to make statistical comparisons after examining the data. One *post hoc* test, the Tukey Honestly Significant Difference (Tukey HSD) allows you to make all *pairwise comparisons*.

An effect size index, f, gives you additional information that the F test doesn't provide. The text's formula for f is appropriate when the sample N's are equal. Values of f of 0.10, 0.25 and 0.40 indicate the size of the effect of the independent variable is small, medium or large, respectively.

After conducting an ANOVA, applying subsequent tests, and finding an effect size estimate, your final task is to explain the results of the experiment using the terms of the experiment. This is perhaps the most important part of data analysis!

The ANOVA technique described in your text is appropriate for analyzing quantitative data from independent samples if certain assumptions about the populations hold true. These assumptions are that the population variances are equal and that the populations are normally distributed. In addition, the technique requires that the participants be randomly assigned to levels of the independent variable if cause and effect conclusions between the independent and dependent variables are drawn.

Multiple-Choice Questions _____

1. The person who developed ANOVA was
    (1) W. S. Gosset, a businessman;
    (2) John W. Tukey, a statistician;
    (3) "student," a pseudonym;
    (4) Ronald A. Fisher, a biologist.

Chapter 10

2. An *F* distribution is a
   (1)   normal distribution;
   (2)   *t* distribution;
   (3)   sampling distribution;
   (4)   none of the above.

3. The null hypothesis tested by ANOVA is that
   (1)   all samples have the same mean;
   (2)   each sample is drawn from a different population;
   (3)   the populations from which the samples are drawn have the same mean;
   (4)   one or more of the populations from which the samples are drawn has a mean that is different from the others.

4. The ANOVA technique described in the text can be used on
   (1)   paired-samples designs;
   (2)   independent-samples designs;
   (3)   both (1) and (2);
   (4)   neither (1) nor (2).

5. If the null hypothesis is true, _____ will be a good estimate of the population variance.
   (1)   the error mean square;
   (2)   the treatment mean square;
   (3)   both (1) and (2);
   (4)   neither (1) nor (2).

6. If the null hypothesis is false, _____ will be a good estimate of the population variance.
   (1)   the error mean square;
   (2)   the treatment mean square;
   (3)   both (1) and (2);
   (4)   neither (1) nor (2).

Chapter 10

7. The larger the population variance, the larger _____ is (are).
   (1) F;
   (2) df_{treat};
   (3) MS_{error};
   (4) all of the above.

8. If a tabled value of F is 10.00 and the F obtained from the data is only 9.00, you should
   (1) retain the null hypothesis;
   (2) reject the null hypothesis;
   (3) calculate the F value again, such a number is not possible;
   (4) not enough information is given.

9. Suppose MS_{treat} is calculated for three samples that are drawn from a population with a mean μ. Under which condition below would MS_{treat} certainly become larger?
   (1) the addition of a sample from a population with the same mean μ;
   (2) the addition of a sample from a population with a mean $\mu + \mu$;
   (3) both (1) and (2);
   (4) the removal of one of the three samples from the calculations.

10. According to the data analyzed and interpreted by your text, the effect of different schedules of reinforcement is to produce different
   (1) speeds of learning during training;
   (2) degrees of persistence during extinction;
   (3) degrees of forgetting over time;
   (4) rates of responding when a maze-learning task is.

11. For a one-way ANOVA an effect size index that qualifies as large is
   (1) 0.20;
   (2) 0.40;
   (3) both (1) and (2);
   (4) neither (1) nor (2).

Chapter 10

12. A group of 72 subjects was equally divided into four groups. A Tukey HSD test produced a value that led to the conclusion that Mean 1 was significantly larger than Mean 2, $p < .05$. Which of the following situations would lead to such a conclusion?
   (1) $\bar{X}_1 = 7$, $\bar{X}_2 = 0$, $MS_{error} = 80$; 3.32
   (2) $\bar{X}_1 = 24$, $\bar{X}_2 = 13$, $MS_{error} = 180$; 3.48
   (3) both (1) and (2);
   (4) neither (1) nor (2).

   HSD=3.74

13. A *priori* and *post hoc* are terms that refer to
   (1) whether the null hypothesis should be rejected;
   (2) whether the assumptions of ANOVA have been met;
   (3) kinds of tests used after an ANOVA;
   (4) all of the above.

14. The Tukey Honestly Significant Difference test is a(n) _____ test.
   (1) a *priori*;
   (2) *post hoc*;
   (3) both (1) and (2);
   (4) neither (1) nor (2).

15. A group of 36 subjects was equally divided into three groups. A Tukey HSD produced a value that led to the conclusion that Mean 1 was significantly larger than Mean 2, $p < .05$. Which of the following situations would lead to such a conclusion?
   (1) $\bar{X}_1 = 9$, $\bar{X}_2 = 2$, $MS_{error} = 50$; 3.43
   (2) $\bar{X}_1 = 24$, $\bar{X}_2 = 14$, $MS_{error} = 84$; 3.78
   (3) both (1) and (2);
   (4) neither (1) nor (2).

   HSD = 3.49

16. Suppose the following F values were calculated from different experiments. If $\alpha = .01$, which of them would lead to rejection of the null hypothesis?
   (1) $F = 18.50$, $df = 2, 2$; ✓
   (2) $F = 2.55$, $df = 10, 17$; ✓
   (3) $F = 2.41$, $df = 20, 42$;
   (4) none of the above.

Chapter 10

17. Compare the *F* test and the *t* test.
    - (1)   The *F* test can be used with only two groups; the *t* test can be used with more than two groups;
    - (2)   The *t* test can be used with only two groups; the *F* test can be used with more than two groups;
    - (3)   There is no difference in number of groups.

18. How many degrees of freedom is there for the numerator and denominator respectively if there are four groups with eight participants in each?
    - (1)   4; 8;
    - (2)   3; 8;
    - (3)   3; 21;
    - (4)   4; 21.

    None! ✻ 3, 28

19. How many degrees of freedom is there for numerator and denominator respectively if there are 3 groups with 10 participants in each?
    - (1)   3, 10;
    - (2)   2, 9;
    - (3)   3, 30;
    - (4)   2, 27.

    2, 27

    $K-1$
    $N_{tot} - K$

20. The difference between the Tukey HSD and *a priori* comparisons is related to
    - (1)   when you decided to make the comparisons;
    - (2)   the type of statistic used;
    - (3)   the power of the statistic;
    - (4)   all of the above.

Interpretation _____

1. Florence Nightingale (1820-1910) was instrumental in reforming medical care. Her methods were based on her experience administering hospitals for British soldiers who were casualties when England was fighting in Crimea (a peninsula in the Black Sea). Part of Nightingale's success can be attributed to her pioneering use of statistics and graphs. (Nightingale was especially appreciative of the earlier work of Quetelet. See Cohen [1984].)

Chapter 10

The "improvement scores" below will produce conclusions like those that Nightingale found when she compared patients in her military hospital in Crimea with civilian patients in English and French hospitals.

Begin by identifying the independent and dependent variable. Next, examine the summary data and calculate F, f, and HSD values. Finally, write your conclusions.

	Hospitals Located in		
	Crimea	England	France
Means	15	9	8
N	12	12	12

Source	Df	MS
Hospitals	2	124.52
Error	33	20.62

2. What affects thinking? Alice Isen's participants worked on seven difficult problems that required creative thinking. One group prepared by exercising; a second group watched a comedy video; a third group simply began working on the problems. The summary statistics that follow include the mean number of problems worked by each group, the ANOVA summary table, f, and the three HSD values. Identify the independent and dependent variable, and write an interpretation of the results.

		Exercise	Comedy	Control
Group Means		2.4	5.1	1.9

Source	SS	df	MS	F	p
Treatments	43.14	2	21.57	8.94	< .01
Error	43.43	18	2.41		
Total	86.57	20			

$f = 0.50$

HSD (Exercise and Comedy) = 4.62
HSD (Exercise and Control) = 0.97
HSD (Comedy and Control) = 5.57

3. A vintner wanted to market a new red wine that would be a blend of several varieties grown in his vineyards. He developed four blends, and he wanted to decide which was the best. He employed the services of eight wine tasters and had each one rate each of the four wines on a 7-point scale, ranging from abominable (1) to exquisite (7). Explain why the ANOVA method described in Chapter 10 is inappropriate for the analysis of the data.

4. Assume that five groups of rats each receive different dosages of a drug. You believe that the dosages are going to result in different running rates among the rats. Further assume that you believe that the rats getting the highest dosage of the drug will run faster than rats receiving the lowest dosage of the drug. What type of analysis will allow you to determine if your belief is correct?

5. What is the difference between ANOVA and the t test? Is there a case where you could use either one? Why or why not?

Problems_____

1. As you know from the text, the time required to extinguish a response depends on the schedule of reinforcement during learning. Extinction time also depends on the predictability of the reinforcement during learning. The following data are patterned after a classic study by Hulse (1973) who reported on the effects of predictability. In this study all pigeons pecked an average of four times for each reinforcement, but the predictability of a reinforcement varied for the three groups. The Very Predictable group was on an FR4 schedule—every fourth response was reinforced. (This is one of the schedules used in the text problem.) The Fairly Predictable group got a reinforcement after two, then four, then six responses. The pattern then repeated. The Unpredictable group was on a schedule produced by a random number generator. It was programmed, however, so that on the average, every fourth response was reinforced. (The name of this schedule is variable

Chapter 10

ratio—4, abbreviated as VR4.) After ten days of training, extinction began (responses were never again reinforced). The time to extinction in minutes was recorded. Identify the independent and dependent variable. Analyze the data as completely as you can and write a conclusion about the predictability of reinforcement and persistence.

Very Predictable	Fairly Predictable	Unpredictable
8	16	18
13	11	19
11	15	22
8		16
		15

2. Farmer Marc A., who also serves as his community's Shakespearean promoter, delivered a plea at the county fair, asking farmers from the county's three groups to lend him unshelled corn. (After examining the groups, you might be able to figure out how he would phrase his plea.) The number of bushels offered by the farmers is shown below. Analyze the data as thoroughly as you can, and write a conclusion about the three groups.

Friends	Romans	Countrymen
7	8	10
9	7	12
3	4	16
5	7	14

3. In most hospital delivery rooms, newborn infants are evaluated at one minute of age and again at five minutes of age. The evaluation is based on the *Apgar Scale*, which uses certain criteria to rate the infant's heart rate, respiratory effort, crying, muscle tone, and color. Scores from 0 to 10 are possible, with 10 indicating the highest general well-being. For the study that is described, the neonate's *Apgar* Score is the dependent variable.

Chapter 10

The independent variable is the type of anesthetic given to the mother: twilight sleep induced by sedatives, spinal block, opiate, and the Lamaze method (no drugs). Below are summary data for the five-minute *Apgar* scores for the newborns.

Perform an ANOVA, calculate F, and make any appropriate HSD tests. Write an interpretation of the results.

	Sedatives	Spinal	Opiate	Lamaze
ΣX	49	74	78	83
ΣX^2	269	574	636	711
N	10	10	10	10

4. Walking is valuable exercise. Is there any relationship between the amount of walking people do and the size of the place where they live? The following summary data (in miles per day) are entirely hypothetical, but they represent what may be the case. Identify the independent and dependent variables, and analyze the scores with an ANOVA and HSD tests. Write a conclusion based on the data. Do you agree with the hypothesis about city/town size and walking? (The place names are ordered from large to small and are from specific sources—can you identify a source or two?)

	Gotham	Middletown	Grovers Corners
ΣX	16	24	32
ΣX^2	70	60	140
N	4	12	8

5. Let's say you are interested in determining if students learn better by hearing about material prior to lecture rather than the traditional way of reading prior to class. Three classes participate in the study. One class has no lecture. They simply read the material. Class two is lectured to after reading the material and class three is lectured to first. You obtain the following data.

Chapter 10

No lecture	Lecture after	Lecture before
.26	.40	.85
.29	.47	.88
.33	.44	.70
.15	.37	.79
.28	.57	.90

What analysis would be appropriate? Would you support the hypothesis that harder work results in better memory? Why or why not?

CHAPTER 11

Analysis of Variance: Factorial Design

Summary_____

A *factorial design* has one dependent variable and two or more independent variables called factors. Each level of one factor is paired with every level of the other factor. A factorial ANOVA tests three null hypotheses: one for each of the two independent variables and one for the interaction between the two independent variables.

Table 11.1 shows a 2 × 3 factorial design. Each participant receives one level of one independent variable and one level of the other independent variable. The participants in the upper left-hand cell of Table 11.1 get Level 1 of Factor A and Level 1 of Factor B. Their dependent-variable scores are entered into cell A_1B_1.

		Independent Variable A			
		Level 1	Level 2	Level 3	Means
	Level 1	Participant's scores	Participant's scores	Participant's scores	$\overline{X}_{B_1}$
Independent Variable B					
	Level 2	Participant's scores	Participant's scores	Participant's scores	$\overline{X}_{B_2}$
	Means	$\overline{X}_{A_1}$	$\overline{X}_{A_2}$	$\overline{X}_{A_3}$	

Table 11.1   Illustration of a 2 × 3 Factorial Design

Table 11.1 also shows marginal means for Factor A and marginal means for Factor B. The means for Factor A (and) are used in *one* of the statistical tests that a factorial ANOVA produces, the main effect of Factor A. The marginal means for Factor B (and) are involved in a *second* statistical test, the main effect of Factor B.

Chapter 11

Each main effect is comparable to a one-way ANOVA, and may be interpreted in the same way as a one-way ANOVA, unless the interaction is significant.

The *third test* in a factorial ANOVA is for an interaction between the two independent variables. Interactions occur when the effect of changing levels of one independent variable depends upon which level of the other independent variable you are administering. That is, one independent variable influences the effect that a second independent variable has on the dependent variable.

Perhaps an example of a significant interaction will help. The effect of chilling a rat until its body temperature is 20°C (37°C is normal) is disastrous; the rat dies. Likewise, asphyxiating a rat causes death. What chance would you predict for a rat undergoing asphyxiation while its body temperature is lowered to 20°C? The usual prediction is $(death)^2$. For these circumstances, however, there is an interaction; the rat lives for a very long time under these conditions. Each condition separately would kill the animal, but together they do not kill. Table 11.2 presents these results using the format of a 2 × 2 factorial design.

		Body Temperature	
		37°C	20°C
Asphyxiation	No	Alive	Dead
	Yes	Dead	Alive

Table 11.2 Illustration of a Significant Interaction

The effect of changing from 37°C to 20 °C depends on whether or not the animal is being asphyxiated. If the animal is not being asphyxiated, changing from 37°C to 20 °C kills it. If the animal is being asphyxiated, the effect is just the opposite; changing from 37°C to 20 °C restores life. To sum up, there is significant interaction in Table 11.2; the effect of asphyxiation depends on body temperature.

Graphs of the cell means are helpful when interpreting the results of a factorial ANOVA. Line graph curves that are not parallel *may* indicate that an interaction has occurred. Likewise, bar graphs with stair steps that change size or direction *may* indicate that two independent variables interact.

Chapter 11

To make the three statistical tests that a factorial ANOVA allows, the total variability of all the scores is partitioned into four components. One component is the variability that is due to one of the factors. A second component is the variability due to the second factor. A third component is the variability due to the interaction. The final component is the error variability, which serves as an estimate of the population variability. Each of these components, divided by its degrees of freedom, results in a mean square. Finally, the error mean square is divided into the mean square for one factor (a main effect), the mean square for the second factor (a second main effect), and into the mean square for interaction (the interaction effect). These divisions produce F values, which are interpreted using a table of the sampling distribution of F.

Tukey HSD tests may be used to make pairwise comparisons among the levels of a factor. These tests can be conducted for either or for both of the factors in a factorial ANOVA. In Table 11.1, a Tukey HSD test on Factor B is unnecessary; the F test on that factor tells you whether or not the two margin means are significantly different. Unfortunately, Tukey HSD tests are not appropriate if the interaction is significant.

Factorial design data can be analyzed with a factorial ANOVA if the dependent variable scores meet certain qualifications. These *assumptions* include the three that must be met by all data analyzed by ANOVA. These assumptions are that the populations the samples are from be *normally distributed* and have *equal variances*, and that *random assignment* (or random sampling) be used. In addition to these assumptions, the methods described in Chapter 11 require that the N's in each cell be equal, that the scores be independent (not paired or related), and that the levels of the independent variable be chosen by the experimenter rather than at random.

Multiple-Choice Questions _____

1. As used in analysis of variance, the term factor means
   - (1) independent variable;
   - (2) dependent variable;
   - (3) extraneous variable;
   - (4) none of the above.

Chapter 11

2. Designs that are equal in the number of factors are
       (1) Independent-samples t test and factorial ANOVA;
       (2) paired-samples t test and factorial ANOVA;
       (3) one-way ANOVA and factorial ANOVA;
       (4) none of the above.

3. A social psychologist was interested in the effect of propaganda on attitudes of males and females. He measured attitudes toward democracy for all participants, delivered the propaganda, and remeasured attitudes toward democracy. He wanted to analyze the data using a 2 × 2 factorial with gender as one independent variable and before-and-after attitudes as the other. The techniques presented in the text will not permit this because
       (1) the scores are not independent;
       (2) an independent variable was not defined ;
       (3) the dependent variable was not defined;
       (4) the levels of the independent variable were not chosen at random by the experimenter.

4. A cell in a factorial ANOVA, refers to
       (1) one level of the independent variable;
       (2) one level of the dependent variable;
       (3) one level of one independent variable and one level of a second independent variable;
       (4) all the participants in the experiment.

5. When the cell means of a factorial design are presented as a line graph, a nonsignificant interaction is indicated by
       (1) parallel lines;
       (2) crossed lines;
       (3) values of F less than 1.00;
       (4) any of the above.

Chapter 11

6. Suppose you had a 2 × 2 factorial ANOVA with the four cell means and you knew that N was 6 for each cell. With this information you could not calculate

    (1) SS_A;
    (2) SS_B;
    (3) SS_B;
    (4) SS_{error}.

7. A 3 x 5 factorial ANOVA has _____ independent variables.

    (1) 1;
    (2) 2;
    (3) 3;
    (4) 5.

8. In a 4 × 4 factorial design with five subjects per cell, the df for the interaction F would be

    $df_{AB} = (k_A - 1)(k_B - 1) = (3)(3) = 9$

    (1) 3, 70 df;
    (2) 6, 64 df;
    $df_{error} = N_{tot} - (A)(B) = 80 - (4)(4) = 64$
    (3) 9, 64 df;
    (4) none of the above.

9. The term *main effect* refers to a comparison of

    (1) means;
    (2) interactions;
    (3) both (1) and (2);
    (4) neither (1) nor (2).

10. An interaction means that

    (1) the cell means all differed;
    (2) the margin means were identical;
    (3) there was a difference between two variables;
    (4) none of the above accurately describe an interaction.

Chapter 11

11. Mr. Jefferson, a farmer-philosopher-president, has a vineyard. On his fields 5-10-5 fertilizer (5 percent nitrogen, 10 percent potash, 5 percent potassium) causes a 10 percent increase in yield. 10-20-10 fertilizer causes a 15 percent increase in yield. Suppose both fertilizers were applied by Mr. Jefferson (whose philosophy is, "If a little bit does a little good, a whole lot will do a lot of good"). Which outcome below would indicate there was no interaction?
   (1) 10 percent increase;
   (2) 15 percent increase;
   (3) either (1) or (2);
   (4) 25 percent increase.

12. "The means of the populations from which the samples were drawn are identical." This is a statement
   (1) of the null hypothesis;
   (2) of one of the assumptions required of data analyzed with a factorial ANOVA;
   (3) about an interaction;
   (4) none of the above

13. Which of the following is (are) true?
   (1) $df_A + df_B = df_{AB}$;
   (2) $MS_A + MS_B = MS_{AB}$;
   (3) both (1) and (2);
   (4) neither (1) nor (2).

14. In common with one-way ANOVA, factorial ANOVA has which of the following assumptions:
   (1) the dependent variable is assumed to be normally distributed;
   (2) the population variances of all the populations samples are equal;
   (3) both (1) and (2);
   (4) neither (1) nor (2).

15. One difference between the one-way ANOVA and factorial ANOVA is that
    (1) factorial ANOVA has two or more dependent variables;
    (2) factorial ANOVA has an independent variable with more than 2 levels;
    (3) factorial ANOVA has two independent variables;
    (4) factorial ANOVA requires fewer assumptions about the data.

16. Suppose a 5 × 6 factorial ANOVA with 7 scores per cell produced $MS_A = 25$, $MS_B = 30$, $MS_{AB} = 15$, and $MS_{error} = 10$ (where A is the 5 in the 5 × 6). With α = .01, a Tukey HSD $F_{01}(20, 120) = 2.06$
    (1) is not appropriate in this instance;
    (2) would be significant for a difference of 2.00 between two A means;
    (3) would be significant for a difference of 2.40 between two A means;
    (4) both (2) or (3).

17. Suppose a 2 × 4 factorial ANOVA with 5 scores per cell produced $MS_A = 200$, $MS_B = 285$, $MS_{AB} = 225$, and $MS_{error} = 100$ (where B is the 4 in the 2 × 4). With α = .01, a Tukey HSD
    (1) is not appropriate in this instance;
    (2) would be significant for a difference of 10 between two B means;
    (3) would be significant for a difference of 15 between two B means;
    (4) neither (2) nor (3).

18. Which of the following would be reason enough not to calculate a Tukey HSD?
    (1) a significant interaction;
    (2) a significant main effect;
    (3) either (1) or (2);
    (4) neither (1) nor (2).

19. A follow-up Tukey HSD is not necessary for main effects when the F value is based on _____ degrees of freedom.
    (1) 1, 20;
    (2) 2, 20;
    (3) 4, 20;
    (4) 4, 10.

Chapter 11

20. Consider a factorial ANOVA in which the dependent variable is reaction time scores. Three different drugs are tested on both females and males. The researchers concluded that the effect of a drug did not depend on whether a person taking it was a female or male. The factorial ANOVA would certainly show that
    (1) there is no main effect for drug;
    (2) there is no main effect for gender;
    (3) there is no interaction;
    (4) all of the above.

Interpretation _____

1. The numbers are cell means. For each figure, indicate whether the interaction and the main effects are not significant or probably significant.

X

	B_1	B_2	B_3
A_1	5	10	15	$\bar{x}=10$
A_2	5	10	15	$\bar{x}=10$

$\bar{x}=5$ $\bar{x}=10$ $\bar{x}=15$

AB Interaction   NO
A Main Effect   NO
B Main Effect   Yes

Y

	B_1	B_2	B_3
A_1	15	10	15	12.5
A_2	5	10	5	7.5

10   10   10

AB Interaction   Yes
A Main Effect   Yes
B Main Effect   NO

2. The numbers are cell means. For each figure, indicate whether the interaction and the main effects are not significant or probably significant.

X

	B_1	B_2
A_1	5	10
A_2	10	5

AB Interaction   _____
A Main Effect   _____
B Main Effect   _____

Y

AB Interaction   _____

	B₁	B₂
A₁	5	10
A₂	5	10

A Main Effect _____

B Main Effect _____

Z

	B₁	B₂
A₁	5	5
A₂	5	10

AB Interaction _____

A Main Effect _____

B Main Effect _____

3. For each figure, indicate whether the interaction and the main effects are not significant or probably significant.

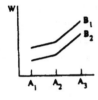

AB Interaction   NO

A Main effect   Yes

B Main effect   Yes

AB Interaction   Yes

A Main effect   NO

B Main effect   ~~NO~~ Yes

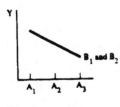

AB Interaction   NO

A Main effect   ~~NO~~ Yes

B Main effect   NO

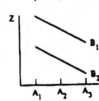

AB Interaction   NO

A Main effect   Yes

B Main effect   ~~NO~~ Yes

Chapter 11

4. For each figure, indicate whether the interaction and the main effects are not significant or probably significant.

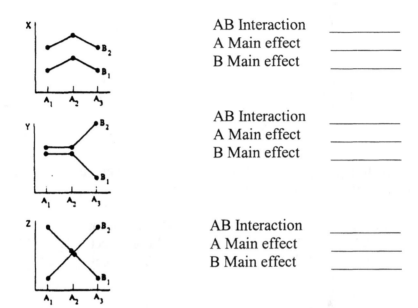

AB Interaction _____
A Main effect   _____
B Main effect   _____

AB Interaction _____
A Main effect   _____
B Main effect   _____

AB Interaction _____
A Main effect   _____
B Main effect   _____

5. Milton Rokeach thinks that racial and ethnic prejudice occurs, not because of differences in race and ethnicity, but because people assume that others differ in basic values. Studies similar to the following have been done to test Rokeach's hypothesis.

Participants were measured on prejudice and then separated into low scorers, moderate scorers, and high scorers. Next, participants read descriptions of people and for each person, they indicated the degree of intimacy they might expect to have with that person. Half the participants read descriptions of persons who differed from themselves in race but not in values; the other half read descriptions that differed in values but not in race. The design is a 2 x 3 factorial. Identify the independent and dependent variables. Examine the summary data that follow and write a description of what the data show.

Chapter 11

		Low (A_1)	Prejudice (A) Moderate (A_2)	High (A_3)
Descriptions	Values(B_1)	8.20	9.00	10.40
Differ (B)	Race (B_2)	15.40	13.40	7.00

Source	SS	df	MS	F	p
Prejudice (A)	54.07	2	27.03	7.51	< .01
Descriptions (B)	56.03	1	56.03	15.56	< .01
AB	150.87	2	75.43	20.95	< .01
Error	86.40	24	3.60		
Total	347.37	29			

6. A social psychologist recruited 30 male and female undergraduates to engage in a telephone conversation with a person of the opposite sex. Afterwards, the participants rated the person "as a person" on a 10-point scale. Each conversation in the experiment was with a confederate of the psychologist. Before the conversation, each participant was given a description of the other person, and embedded in the description was the second independent variable: physical attractiveness. The descriptions included one of three phrases, "truly gorgeous," "kind of ordinary looking," or "pretty ugly, really." Examine the table of cell means and the ANOVA summary table. Write an explanation of what the data show.

Chapter 11

	Gender	
	Males (A₁)	Females (A₂)
Gorgeous (B₁)	8.10	8.00
Ordinary (B₂)	6.10	6.50
Ugly (B₃)	4.60	4.70

Source	SS	df	MS	F	p
Gender (A)	.27	1	.27	0.09	$> .05$
Description (B)	115.63	2	57.82	18.50	$< .01$
AB	.63	2	.32	0.10	$> .05$
Error	168.80	54	3.13		
Total	285.33	59			

Problems _____

1. Carl Hovland (Hovland, Lumsdaine, & Sheffield, 1949) conducted a study during WW II to find out whether people were more likely to be persuaded by a message that gave just one side of an issue or by one that gave both sides. (In 1944, Germany was falling, and the attitude of many American soldiers was that the war with Japan would soon be over. Afraid that battle preparedness would fall off, the Army wanted to reverse this attitude. The question was "How should we present the argument?") In one part of Hovland's study, there were two independent variables—number of sides of the argument presented and educational level of the listeners. The dependent variable was the amount of attitude change produced. Below are summary data. Finish the analysis, and interpret the results.

	High School Graduate	
	Yes (A_1)	No (A_2)
One-sided Argument (B_1)	$\Sigma X_{A1B1} = 64$ $\Sigma X^2_{A1B1} = 808$ $N = 6$	$\Sigma X_{A2B1} = 123$ $\Sigma X^2_{A2B1} = 2603$ $N = 6$
Two-sided (B_2)	$\Sigma X_{A1B2} = 64$ $\Sigma X^2_{A1B2} = 808$ $N = 6$	$\Sigma X_{A2B2} = 64$ $\Sigma X^2_{A2B2} = 808$ $N = 6$

2. Two approaches to learning a list of words are rote rehearsal and elaborative rehearsal. In rote rehearsal, a person repeats the word over and over. Some words such as truck and rose have high imagery and others such as honor and concept have low imagery. For elaborative rehearsal, a person gets a mental image or association to a word. The data below show the number of words correctly recalled from a list after using one of the rehearsal techniques. Perform a factorial ANOVA, compile a summary table, and write a conclusion.
   High Imagery, Rote Strategy: 8, 6, 5, 6
   High Imagery, Elaborative Strategy: 13, 10, 8, 15
   Low Imagery, Rote Strategy: 6, 5, 3, 4
   Low Imagery, Elaborative Strategy: 7, 5, 2, 3

CHAPTER 12

Analysis of Variance: One-Factor Repeated Measures

Summary _____

The design described in this chapter is the analysis-of-variance version of the paired-samples t test. The only difference is that a *one-factor repeated measures ANOVA* can analyze *more* than two levels of the independent variable; a t test can analyze *only* two levels.

Like a one-way ANOVA, a one-factor repeated measures ANOVA has *one independent variable* (factor) that has two or more levels and there is *one dependent variable*. However, with a one-factor repeated measures ANOVA, there is a reason to match up the scores in the different treatments. Reasons might be that the same person contributed a score to each of the treatments or that a sub-group of participants (equal in size to the number of treatments) was alike on some matching variable.

In a display of the data for a one-factor repeated measures ANOVA, columns represent the treatments and rows represent the matched participants. A one-factor repeated measures ANOVA partitions the total variance in the dependent variable scores among *three* identifiable sources. One source is the variability due to the independent variable (columns); degrees of freedom are $N_K - 1$. A second source is the variance that is due to participants (rows); $df = N_t - 1$. The third source is the variance that remains (the error variance) $df = (N_K - 1)(N_t - 1)$. The F test, which determines if there are any significant differences among the treatment means, is a ratio of the mean square for the treatments divided by the mean square for error.

As a comparison, a one-way ANOVA partitions the total variance into only two sources, a treatment variance and an error variance. A one-factor repeated measures ANOVA, however, removes the effect of participants from the total variance, which makes it more sensitive than a one-way ANOVA. The variance is removed because in the one-factor repeated measures ANOVA, there should be minimum variance between conditions due to participants. This is because participants are either matched on some specific, important criteria, or because they are the same participant.

Chapter 12

One advantage of one-factor repeated measures ANOVA is that it is more *efficient;* that is, it requires less time and effort to obtain a given number of scores. A *second advantage* is that it is more *powerful* because the error variance is smaller. The error variance is smaller because the variance due to the participants has been removed. A *disadvantage* of a one-factor repeated measures ANOVA is that it may contain unwanted *carryover* effects.

Like other ANOVA designs in previous chapters, pairwise comparisons among the several treatments can be made with Tukey *HSD* tests.

Type I and Type II errors were explained again. Type I errors occur when you reject a true null hypothesis and a Type II error occurs when you retain a false null hypothesis.

Two of the mathematical *assumptions* of one-factor repeated measures ANOVA are that the population scores are normally distributed and that the data show covariance matrix sphericity, a concept that was not explained due to its mathematical complexity.

Multiple-Choice Questions _____

Data Set 12-1. Work carefully—one error can cause more than one question to be missed.

Participants	X_1	X_2	X_3	Σ
1	2	3	7	12
2	3	5	6	14
Σ	5	8	13	26

1. In Data Set 12-1, SS_{tot} is equal to
    (1) 19.33;
    (2) 106.00;
    (3) 127.67;
    (4) none of the above; answer is _____.

Chapter 12

2. In Data Set 12-1, SS_{treat} is equal to
   - (1) 0.67;
   - (2) 16.33;
   - (3) 124.67;
   - (4) none of the above; answer is _____.

3. In Data Set 12-1, MS_{error} is equal to
   - (1) 2.33;
   - (2) 1.50;
   - (3) 1.17;
   - (4) none of the above; answer is _____.

4. In Data Set 12-1, the F value for a repeated-measures ANOVA is
   - (1) 3.50;
   - (2) 4.44;
   - (3) 10.20;
   - (4) none of the above; answer is _____.

5. A repeated-measures ANOVA removes _____ variance from further consideration in the analysis.
   - (1) between treatments;
   - (2) between subjects;
   - (3) error;
   - (4) all of the above.

6. The F ratio in a repeated-measures ANOVA consists of the
   - (1) between-subjects variance divided by the between-treatments variance;
   - (2) between-treatments variance divided by the between-subjects variance;
   - (3) between-subjects variance divided by the error variance;
   - (4) between-treatments variance divided by the error variance.

Chapter 12

7. A one-factor repeated-measures ANOVA is like a one-way ANOVA with respect to
    (1) the number of pieces that the total variance is partitioned into;
    (2) its efficiency;
    (3) its power;
    (4) none of the above.

8. The number of independent variables that can be handled by a one-factor repeated-ANOVA
    (1) is 1;
    (2) is 2;
    (3) is 3;
    (4) depends on the number of levels of the independent variable.

9. A one-factor repeated-measures ANOVA partitions the total variance into _____ component(s).
    (1) 1;
    (2) 2;
    (3) 3;
    (4) 4.

10. An *F* value of 3.50 with 4 and 10 degrees of freedom is obtained from the data. You should _____ the null hypothesis, even though you might be making a _____ error.
    (1) reject; Type I;
    (2) reject; Type II;
    (3) retain; Type I;
    (4) retain; Type II;

11. Which answer first defines a Type I error and then a Type II error?
    (1) retain a false null hypothesis; reject a true null hypothesis;
    (2) retain a false null hypothesis; retain a true null hypothesis;
    (3) reject a false null hypothesis; retain a true null hypothesis;
    (4) reject a true null hypothesis; retain a false null hypothesis.

Chapter 12

12. For which of the descriptions that follow would a repeated-measures ANOVA not be appropriate? A study in which
          (1) the population variances are quite different;
          (2) there are carryover effects from one administration of one level of the independent variable to the next;
          (3) both of the above;
          (4) neither of the above.

13. The advantages listed by your text for a repeated-measures ANOVA were
          (1) accuracy and elegance;
          (2) precision and adaptability;
          (3) efficiency and power;
          (4) simplicity and congruence.

14. A disadvantage of the repeated-measures ANOVA described in your text is that you cannot
          (1) make pairwise tests after the F test;
          (2) test the significance of the between-subjects term;
          (3) test more than three levels of the independent variable;
          (4) all of the above.

15. What is the critical value for a repeated-measures ANOVA that has three subjects who provide data for four conditions? Let $\alpha = .05$.
          (1) 3.84;
          (2) 4.76;
          (3) 5.14;
          (4) none of the above.

16. Which of the following is an advantage of a repeated-measures ANOVA over one-way ANOVA?
          (1) The repeated-measures ANOVA is more efficient;
          (2) The repeated-measures ANOVA eliminates variance due to participants;
          (3) The repeated-measures ANOVA is more powerful;
          (4) All are advantages.

17. With a repeated-measures ANOVA, error variance due to subjects is lower because
    (1) the subjects are matched on some variable;
    (2) the subjects are the same people in different conditions;
    (3) both (1) and (2) could be correct;
    (4) neither (1) nor (2) can be correct.

18. Theoretically, the difference between a one-way ANOVA and a repeated-measures ANOVA is that
    (1) the one-way ANOVA is more powerful;
    (2) the repeated-measures ANOVA is more powerful;
    (3) there is no difference in power;
    (4) not enough information to answer the question.

19. A psychologist finds a significant difference between two conditions. She is very happy, and decides to repeat the study. This time, she finds no significant difference. Suppose she runs the study ten additional times, and fails to find a significant difference. There is a good chance that the significant difference she found the first time was due to
    (1) Type I error;
    (2) Type II error;
    (3) either Type I or Type II error;
    (4) neither Type I nor Type II error.

20. Type II errors are made when the researcher
    (1) rejects the null hypothesis when it shouldn't be rejected;
    (2) retains the null hypothesis when it shouldn't be rejected;
    (3) rejects the null hypothesis when it should be rejected;
    (4) retains the null hypothesis when it should be rejected.

Short Answer Questions _____

1. List all the advantages you can think of for using a repeated-measures design over an independent group design. If you were to design a study using a repeated-measure design, what would be your main concern?

Chapter 12

2. Design a repeated-measures experiment. In doing so, identify independent and dependent variables, hypotheses and statement of the problem.

Problems _____

1. A classic study describe in a previous chapter taught us that our memories vary depending on the level at which we process information. Craik and Tulving (1975) presented nouns visually to participants for 0.2 seconds and later had them recognize as many as they could. Before each noun was presented, one of three kinds of questions was posed. To get an answer these three kinds of questions required different levels of processing. Examples of these three levels were:

"Was the word in capital letters?"—shallow processing

"Does the word rhyme with train?"—medium processing

"Does the word fit in this sentence, 'The girl put the _____ on the table'?"—deep processing

The proportions of presented words that were recognized in each condition are shown in the table, which was constructed to produce mean proportions like those found by Craik and Tulving. Analyze the scores with a repeated-measures ANOVA and make all three pairwise comparisons with Tukey *HSD* tests. Write an interpretation.

| | Level of Processing | | |
Participant	Shallow	Medium	Deep
1	5	40	90
2	30	60	80
3	10	50	85
4	8	30	85
5	22	70	60

Chapter 12

2. T. S. Spatz (1991) conducted workshops teaching women to do breast self examination. She gave participants a 27-item true/false test of their knowledge before they were trained (pretest), after they were trained (posttest), and again three months later (follow-up). The scores below mimic her results. Analyze them with a repeated-measures ANOVA and Tukey *HSD* tests. Write an interpretation.

Participant	Pretest	Posttest	Follow-up
1	7	22	16
2	10	20	22
3	10	23	24
4	13	21	16
5	15	26	22
6	17	26	26

3. A study by O'Brien and his colleagues (O'Brien, Albrecht, Hakala, & Rizzella, 1995) found that participants were able to remember information presented earlier in a text when they were prompted to do so. The information was presented early in the text (first two sentences), the middle of the text (sentence 5-7) or at the end (sentence 9-11). They measured reaction time as an indication of whether or not the participants were thinking about those concepts at the end of the passage. The data below represent reaction time scores in milliseconds. Analyze these data with a repeated-measures ANOVA and pairwise comparisons. Write an interpretation.

Participant	Early	Middle	Late
1	514	521	512
2	525	526	505
3	601	618	609
4	499	492	533
5	537	598	544

CHAPTER 13

The Chi Square Test

Summary _____

Chi square (χ^2) is yet another null hypothesis statistical test (NHST). A chi square test results in a conclusion about the relationship between two variables. Chi square is appropriate when the information on a subject or event is not a qualitative score but the category the subject or event is in. Chi square compares the *observed frequencies (O)* in the categories to *expected frequencies (E)*. The expected frequencies come from a hypothesis about the population that the sample data are from. In every case, ΣO must equal ΣE.

Two kinds of χ^2 tests were described. In an *independence test*, the null hypothesis is that the two variables are independent. A *rejected* null hypothesis means that the two variables are related; they are not independent. A *retained* null hypothesis means that the data support the conclusion that the variables are independent (but independence is *not* proved).

In a *goodness-of-fit* χ^2 test, the null hypothesis comes from a theory. If the null hypothesis is rejected, conclude that the theory *fails* to be consistent with the data. If the null hypothesis is retained, conclude that the theory is in *accord* with the data (but not that the theory is *proved* correct).

If one or more expected frequency is *small* (around 5 or less), the probabilities given by the chi square distribution may not be accurate. The best solution is to gather sufficient data to avoid this problem. A second solution is to combine categories, which results in fewer categories and larger expected frequencies.

Each χ^2 problem has an associated *degrees of freedom*. For tests of independence, (contingency tables of rows and columns), $df = (R-1)(C-1)$. For goodness-of-fit tests with one variable and two or more categories, degrees of freedom is equal to the number of categories minus one. If other restrictions are added to goodness-of-fit tests, one *df* is subtracted for each parameter estimated. An example of a restriction is that of arranging the mean and standard deviation of the

Chapter 13

expected scores so that they are equal to the mean and standard deviation of the observed scores.

The *effect size index* for a 2 x 2 test of independence is phi φ (pronounced "fee"). Small, medium, and large values of φ are 0.10, 0.30, and 0.50 respectively. Chi square tests are appropriate if:

1. the measurement of a subject or event places it into a category.
2. the measurement of one subject or event does not influence the measurement of another subject or event (the measurements must be independent).
3. samples are representative of the populations that the conclusions apply to.

Multiple-Choice Questions _____

1. The person who developed χ^2 was
   (1) Ronald A. Fisher;
   (2) William S. Gosset;
   (3) Karl Pearson;
   (4) Helen Walker.

2. The shape of the theoretical χ^2 distribution is determined by
   (1) the number of observations;
   (2) the size of the expected frequency of events;
   (3) the number of categories of events;
   (4) all of the above.

3. The sum of the expected frequencies must be equal to
   (1) the sum of the observed frequencies;
   (2) the *df*;
   (3) $(R-1)(C-1)$;
   (4) none of the above.

Chapter 13

4. A developmental psychologist developed a theory that predicted the proportion of children who would, in a period of stress, cling to the mother, attack the mother, or attack a younger sibling. The stress situation was set up, and the responses of 50 children were recorded. The appropriate χ^2 test is a test of
    (1) goodness of fit with 2 *df*;
    (2) goodness of fit with 40 *df*;
    (3) independence with 2 *df*;
    (4) independence with 40 *df*.

5. The null hypothesis for a goodness-of-fit test is that the observed frequencies
    (1) fit the expected frequencies;
    (2) do not fit the expected frequencies;
    (3) either (1) or (2), depending of the size of the χ^2 value;
    (4) either (1) or (2), depending on the size of the χ^2 and the *df*.

6. In a χ^2 test of independence between sex and kinds of phobias, the null hypothesis was rejected. The proper conclusion is that
    (1) sex and phobias are independent of each other;
    (2) sex and phobias are related to each other;
    (3) knowing a person's phobia gives you no clue to his or her sex;
    (4) none of the above.

7. A χ^2 test of goodness of fit was used to evaluate a model. The null hypothesis was rejected. The proper conclusion is that the model is
    (1) adequate;
    (2) inadequate;
    (3) either (1) or (2), depending on the *df*;
    (4) models must be evaluated with a test of independence.

8. To use the χ^2 distribution with confidence you must assume that the observations you make
    (1) are normally distributed;
    (2) have equal variances;
    (3) are independent;
    (4) all of the above.

Chapter 13

9. To find expected frequencies in a test of independence,
   (1) begin by assuming that the categories are independent;
   (2) use predictions based on a theory;
   (3) begin by assuming that the categories of events are related in some way;
   (4) none of the above.

10. For a 2×2 χ^2 test of independence, _____ is the effect size index, and _____ is a medium value.
   (1) θ (theta); .50;
   (2) θ (theta); .30;
   (3) φ (phi); .50;
   (4) φ (phi); .30.

11. Suppose you were analyzing data from a 2×2 test of independence and you had one expected frequency that was very small. According to your text you are very likely to make a
   (1) Type I error;
   (2) Type II error;
   (3) both (1) and (2);
   (4) neither (1) nor (2).

12. If you compare chi square curves for skewness, you'll find that as degrees of freedom increase the curves are
   (1) positively skewed but becoming less so;
   (2) positively skewed and becoming more so;
   (3) negatively skewed and becoming less so;
   (4) negatively skewed and becoming more so.

13. After the data are gathered, a statistician may decide to combine logically related categories. The most likely reason for this is to
   (1) hide mistakes;
   (2) increase the size of some expected values;
   (3) increase the degrees of freedom;
   (4) decrease the skew of the chi square distribution.

Chapter 13

14. Being able to examine each group's contribution to the final value of a chi square value was described as being due to the _____ nature of chi square.
    (1) distributive;
    (2) additive;
    (3) combinatorial;
    (4) summative.

15. The result of Cambridge-Somerville Youth Study described in your text was that
    (1) youth from low socioeconomic status homes were twice as likely to have a police record as youth from higher socioeconomic status homes;
    (2) youth from low socioeconomic status homes were no more likely to have a police record than youth from higher socioeconomic status hones;
    (3) youth with counselors and enrichment opportunities were less likely to have a police record than youth without counselors and opportunities;
    (4) youth with counselors and enrichment opportunities were just as likely to have a police record as youth without counselors and opportunities.

16. A friend brings you data that can be used to establish the independence of two variables. You run an analysis on the data and find a chi square value smaller than the tabled value. Your analysis supports the idea that the two variables
    (1) are independent;
    (2) are not independent;
    (3) either (1) or (2) depending whether the calculated value is significantly smaller than the tabled value.

17. The goodness-of-fit test is useful in helping us determine
    (1) whether or not the data fit our hypothesis;
    (2) whether or not our data fit what is expected by chance;
    (3) both (1) and (2);
    (4) neither (1) nor (2).

Chapter 13

18. Assume you are interested in determining if there is a preference in the dining hall for a particular night. You would expect, by chance, that there would be an equal number of students eating in the dining hall each night. You collect the data. Which χ^2 test is MOST appropriate?
    - (1) χ^2 test for independence;
    - (2) goodness of fit;
    - (3) either, depending on degrees of freedom;
    - (4) neither; you should use a t test.

19. Suppose your data produce an effect size estimate of 0.30. According to the text, this is a
    - (1) large effect size;
    - (2) medium effect size;
    - (3) small effect size.

20. For the χ^2 test described in question 18, how many degrees of freedom are there?
    - (1) 8;
    - (2) 7;
    - (3) 6;
    - (4) 12.

Interpretation _____

1. In the study of human origins, anthropologists divide themselves into two camps: the "lumpers" (who argue that the pieces of evidence are not all that different) and the "splitters" (who argue that the differences represent separate species). A budding anthropologist wondered if being a lumper or splitter was related to experience as an anthropologist. She gathered the following data, which produced a χ^2 value of 16.67. Calculate φ and write a conclusion about anthropologists.

	Lumpers	Splitters	Σ
Less than 5 yrs. Experience	10	30	40
More than 5 yrs. Experience	40	20	60
Σ	50	50	

Chapter 13

2. Let's say you collect data on skipping class. You examine male students and female students who have low, medium and high GPA's. You obtain a χ^2 value of 9.96. Write a conclusion about skipping class.

	Low	Medium	High	Σ
Males	35	21	14	70
Females	21	25	31	77
Σ	56	46	45	

Problems _____

1. In an activity-wheel experiment, animals were either isolated or housed together. Both groups were allowed food for one hour each day. After 25 days, the animals were either alive with stabilized weights or they were dead. Test for the independence of these two conditions with a χ^2 test. Calculate φ. Write a conclusion. For the reasoning behind this experiment, see Spatz and Jones (1971).

	Living Conditions	
	Isolated	Together
Alive	10	8
Dead	2	12

2. With tomatoes, the color of the fruit and the height of the plant are genetically determined (with red dominant over yellow, and tall dominant over short). Suppose for a few minutes that you are a geneticist during the 1920s or 1930s when these facts were unknown. If the above facts about dominance are true, a particular set of crossings will result in a 9:3:3:1 ratio, with 9 tall reds to 3 short reds to 3 tall yellows to 1 short yellow. Suppose you carried out the crossings and found 90 tall reds, 39 short reds, 39 tall yellows, and 18 short yellows. Use a χ^2 test to determine if such data fit a 9:3:3:1 model. (Note: 9:3:3:1 is a shortcut way to write 9/16, 3/16, 3/16, 1/16.) Is this a test for independence or goodness of fit?

Chapter 13

3. You may remember a textbook problem that used M&M candy. The answer to that problem suggested that a larger sample would make a more realistic problem. I took the textbook's advice and bought a 22.7 ounce bag of plain M&M's. There were 756 pieces of candy in the bag. The Mars company says that the color distribution in plain M&M's is brown—30%; yellow—20%; red—20%; blue—10%; green—10% orange—10% (www.mms.com/us/about/products/index.jsp). The frequency count in my bag was: brown—222; yellow—149; red—132; blue—102; green—44; orange—107. Identify this problem as a test of independence or of goodness-of-fit. Calculate χ^2 and write an interpretation.

4. A researcher asked 173 people with different educational accomplishments to respond to the statement "Our planet is being observed by intelligent life forms from outer space." Responses were given on a 7-point scale from "Strong Agreement" to "Strong Disagreement." The number of people responding in each educational category follows. Analyze the data, and comment on the relationship between level of education and agreement with the statement.

Level of Agreement	College Educated	High School Dropouts
Strong Agreement	2	4
Mild Agreement	7	10
Slight Agreement	15	24
Neutral	19	21
Slight Disagreement	23	18
Mild Disagreement	12	9
Strong Disagreement	6	3

5. One year just before the end of the 20th century in America, 1,985,596 baby boys and 1,895,298 baby girls were born. Use a chi square test to determine if these data fit the theory that girls and boys are born in equal numbers.

CHAPTER 14

More Nonparametric Tests

Summary _____

To use the nonparametric statistical tests in this chapter, the data must be ranks or be reduced to ranks.

Nonparametric statistics are similar to parametric statistics in some ways and different from them in others. They are similar in that they use the same hypothesis-testing logic (NHST) and that they require random assignment (or random sampling). They are different in that they do not assume that populations are normally distributed or that the variances are equal. They are also different because the null hypothesis is that the population *distributions* are identical rather than that the population *means* are identical.

To test the hypothesis that two population distributions are identical when data are from a two-group, *independent-samples design*, use the *Mann-Whitney U test*. Rank the scores for the entire data set, and then separately sum the ranks for each group. Using these sums in a formula, calculate two values of U. Use the smaller U. For designs with both N's less than 20, U is evaluated for significance with Table H. For larger samples, a z test based on the smaller U is used.

To test the hypothesis that two population distributions are identical when data are from a two-group, *paired-samples design*, use the *Wilcoxon matched-pairs, signed-ranks T test*. The difference between pairs of scores is found. The differences are ranked, with the smallest difference ranked 1. Each rank receives the algebraic sign of its difference. Positive ranks are summed to produce a T value. Negative ranks are summed to produce a second T value. Using the absolute value, the smaller of the two T's is evaluated for significance. If the number of pairs is less than 50, T is evaluated with a Table J. For larger samples, a z test based on the smaller T value is used.

Contrary to other statistical tests you have studied, calculated values for both U and T must be *less* than tabled critical value to be significant.

Chapter 14

To test the hypothesis that population distributions are identical when the data are from an independent-samples design with *more than two levels* of the independent variable, use the *Wilcoxon-Wilcox multiple comparisons test*. Rank the scores for the whole data set and then separately sum the ranks for each group. Find the difference for each pair of groups. Each difference is evaluated for significance with a table of critical differences for the Wilcoxon-Wilcox multiple comparisons test, Table K.

To find the *degree of relationship* between two variables, use the Spearman r_s. Rank the scores within one group and then rank the scores in the other group. Find the difference between the ranks for each pair. Square the differences, sum them, and use this sum of the squared differences in the formula for r_s.

To test the hypothesis that two populations have a correlation coefficient of .00, calculate r_s and evaluate its significance using Table L (for N 16) or Table A (for $N > 16$).

The parametric counterparts of the nonparametric tests in this chapter are:
Mann-Whitney U test – independent-samples t test
Wilcoxon matched-pairs, signed-ranks T test – paired-samples t test
Wilcoxon-Wilcox multiple comparisons test – Tukey HSD test
Spearman r_s – Pearson product-moment correlation coefficient, r

The textbook's final word is that statistical methods and techniques are useful in some situations but not in others. Unfortunately, no practice problems were given to help you sharpen your understanding of this issue. However, knowing what statistics can and cannot do is a good start. We wish you well as you continue to develop your skills.

Multiple-Choice Questions _____

1. The nonparametric tests in the text are based on sampling distributions of
    (1) means;
    (2) mean differences;
    (3) ranks;
    (4) variances.

Chapter 14

2. The nonparametric test that corresponds in design to the independent-samples *t* test is the
   (1) Mann-Whitney U test;
   (2) Wilcoxon matched-pairs singed-ranks T test;
   (3) Wilcoxon-Wilcox multiple-comparisons test;
   (4) r_s.

3. Suppose you find that three people tied for the top score in a Wilcoxon-Wilcox multiple-comparisons test. The correct procedure is to
   (1) assign a rank of 1 to all three;
   (2) assign a rank of 2 to all three;
   (3) assign a rank of 3 to all three;
   (4) randomly determine which scores get ranks 1, 2, and 3.

4. Nonparametric tests are used rather than a *t* test or an ANOVA when
   (1) the researcher does not know the specific value of the population parameters;
   (2) the data are in the form of ranks;
   (3) the assumption of random assignment is not justified;
   (4) both (2) and (3).

5. The null hypothesis for testing the significance of r_s is that the population correlation coefficient is
   (1) .00;
   (2) 1.00;
   (3) the statistic, r_s, calculated from the sample data;
   (4) none of the above.

6. Your text discussed two issues for which hard and fast rules don't exist on the choice of parametric or nonparametric tests. These are:
   (1) random assignment and scales of measurement;
   (2) sample size and power;
   (3) random assignment and sample size;
   (4) scales of measurement and power.

Chapter 14

7. When a sample size is large, the U value from a Mann-Whitney U test is evaluated using the
    (1) t distribution;
    (2) normal distribution;
    (3) F distribution;
    (4) χ^2 distribution.

8. Which of the following statistical tests is most similar to the Mann-Whitney U test?
    (1) t test;
    (2) ANOVA;
    (3) χ^2 test;
    (4) r_s.

9. To test for a significant difference between paired samples, use a
    (1) Mann-Whitney U test;
    (2) Wilcoxon matched-pairs signed-ranks T test;
    (3) Wilcoxon-Wilcox multiple-comparisons test;
    (4) r_s.

10. Which of the following could *not* be analyzed with a Wilcoxon-Wilcox multiple-comparisons test?
    (1) three independent samples;
    (2) $N_1 = 10$, $N_2 = 20$, $N_3 = 30$;
    (3) the data for three groups that consisted of ranks in college;
    (4) all of the above.

11. What is the rank of 4 in the following distribution?
    1, 2, 2, 3, 3, 4, 4, 5, 5.
    (1) 4;
    (2) 5.5;
    (3) 6;
    (4) 7.
    (5) none of the above, answer is _____.

Chapter 14

12. Power is the likelihood of
    (1) rejecting H_o when it is true;
    (2) rejecting H_o when it is false;
    (3) retaining H_o when it is true;
    (4) retaining H_o when it is false.

13. Which of the following factors has an influence on power?
    (1) sample size;
    (2) effect size;
    (3) statistical test;
    (4) all can influence power.

14. Suppose you found, for the 26 people in your wing of the dorm, a Spearman r_s of .38 between the number of breakfasts eaten during the term and grade point average. You may conclude that there is
    (1) no significant relationship;
    (2) a significant relationship at the .05 level;
    (3) a significant relationship at the .01 level;
    (4) a significant relationship at the .001 level.

15. If you have one difference score of 0 it should be kept in the analysis for
    (1) Wilcoxon matched-pairs signed-rank T test;
    (2) Spearman r_s;
    (3) both (1) and (2);
    (4) neither (1) nor (2).

16. One common use of statistics is to compile a composite score for each city on a list of cities. Suppose you thought that large cities would rank higher than small cities. To make sure that the age of the city didn't influence the comparison, you matched each large city with a small one that was founded at about the same time. Which statistic below should you use to test your idea about the size of cities and their rank?
    (1) Mann-Whitney U test;
    (2) Wilcoxon matched-pairs signed-ranks T;
    (3) Wilcoxon-Wilcox multiple comparisons test;
    (4) Spearman's r_s.

Chapter 14

17. Which of the following captures the theme of the E. F. Schumacher anecdote at the end of the book?
    (1) Accurate counting is necessary for statistics;
    (2) Inferential statistics is central to all decision making;
    (3) Nonparametric statistics show that there will be new developments in statistics;
    (4) Some problems are not solved by being translated into numbers.

18. The _____ the value of U and the _____ the value of T, the more likely you are to reject the null hypothesis.
    (1) larger, larger;
    (2) larger, smaller;
    (3) smaller, smaller;
    (4) smaller, larger.

Interpretation _____

1. Which nonparametric test should be used to analyze data from the following studies?
    A. Some experimenters, impressed by the intimidation power of a steady, direct gaze by dominant primates, decided to investigate the effect in *Homo sapiens*. They rode a motor scooter up next to a car stopped at an intersection with a stoplight and either stared directly at the driver or stared ahead. The dependent variable was the time it took the driver to cross the intersection. (Results: staring increases speed for *Homo sapiens* too.)
    B. Countries are ranked on infant mortality rates. Suppose you had the ranks for 15 countries and the rank for each of the countries for population density. What test would determine whether there was a relationship between the two variables?
    C. To determine if there was sex discrimination in salaries at Old State U., a statistician began with 15 female professors. On the basis of degree, discipline, and years of experience, each was matched with a male professor.

Chapter 14

2. Which nonparametric test should be used to analyze data from the following studies?

   A. To produce high-frustration, subjects were forced to wait 15 minutes for a late participant before beginning an experiment. Low-frustration subjects started on time. During the experiment aggression was measured as the dependent variable.

   B. To find out if there was a relationship between a basketball team's height and its rank in the conference, the average height and conference rank were determined for the 10 schools in the Central Collegiate Conference.

   C. In a before-and-after study, participants rated their views on abortion. Between conditions, they watched a propaganda movie.

3. A P. E. instructor designed a CVR (cardiovascular-respiratory) fitness program that gradually increased the duration and intensity of exercise over a 6-month period. The 9 participants in the program were measured for general fitness at the beginning and at the end of the program on such measures as percent body fat, vital lung capacity, and blood pressure and heart rate. Each participant was assigned a "fitness" score on a scale of 1 (a physical disaster) to 10 (superb specimen). A Wilcoxon matched-pairs signed-ranks T test produced a T value of 5.5. Was the program effective in improving CVR fitness?

4. A social psychologist examined the effect of sex education in the public schools. She randomly selected 25 college sophomore women and asked them if they had a sex education course in elementary school. She then asked them to complete a questionnaire concerning their sexual activity. Two refused to complete the questionnaire. She used the questionnaire results to rank-order the women from most (rank = 1) to least (rank = 23) sexually active. The sum of ranks for those who had not had a sex education course (N = 14) was 135. For those who had taken a course (N = 9), the sum was 141. The smaller U value was 30. Complete the analysis and write an interpretation regarding elementary school sex education courses.

Chapter 14

5. Students face the practical question of how to use study time efficiently (that is, how to have more time to play). Gates conducted an early study (1917), which was used as a model for the data that follow. Twenty students were divided into five groups. The students all studied an article on dinosaurs, but each group spent a different proportion of the time in "self-recitation" (looking away from the article and mentally reciting what had been read). Afterward, each student took a 100-point test on the material in the article. The sums of the ranks are shown below. (The best score was ranked 1.) Finish the analysis and write an explanation that the data support.

Proportion of Study Time Spent
in Self-Recitation

0	20	40	60	80
73	54	44.5	27.5	11

6. Work Problem 1 that follows and then come back to this interpretation problem.

In addition to tests that simulated pilots' eye-hand coordination tasks, printed tests were used. A Spearman r_s between a general information test (with items such as, *name the five Great Lakes*) and the pilot competency test was .49. Compare this correlation coefficient to that in Problem 1 and draw a conclusion.

Problems _____

1. During WW II, enlistees were selected for pilot training on the basis of test scores. Some of the tests were printed, and some were eye-hand coordination tests that simulated tasks that pilots actually performed. One important eye-hand coordination test was the pursuit rotor, which requires tracking a target. The data that follow show time on target for the pursuit rotor during the fifth trial of practice and a "pilot competency score," which is based on actual flying skill. Find r_s (which will be the same as that found by Air Force researchers).

Chapter 14

Seconds on Target Max. = 30	Pilot Competency Score
18	37
15	57
28	63
25	41
9	31
17	51
23	42
11	45

2. Many nurses are reluctant to approach patients diagnosed as having psychological problems. To help alleviate the problem, a Director of Nursing developed a training program to change nurses' attitudes toward such patients. To assess the effectiveness of the program, two matched groups were formed. Only one group completed the program, but both groups completed an attitude test. High scores indicate positive attitudes toward patients with psychological problems. Analyze the data with a Wilcoxon matched-pairs signed-ranks T test, and comment on the success or failure of the program.

	Attitude Scores	
Matched Pairs	Untrained	Trained
1	21	23
2	12	18
3	17	22
4	23	23
5	16	17
6	21	24
7	19	27
8	14	13

Chapter 14

3. Karl Lashley carried out a 30-year search for the engram (the physical basis of memory). One of the many variables he studied was *place*. In one study, Lashley removed 40 percent of a rat's brain from either the frontal lobe or the parietal lobe. The following errors were produced by rats when their memory was tested. Analyze them with an appropriate nonparametric test. The sentence explanation you write will be a paraphrase of Lashley's conclusion.

Frontal	Parietal
54	47
31	30
18	12
26	17
39	21
42	25
45	35

4. A consumer advocate compared the cleanliness of four chains of supermarkets by devising a 50-point rating scale and inspecting six stores of each chain. The higher the score, the cleaner the store. Analyze the data, and make your shopping recommendations to the public.

Score	Chain
35	A
39	C
29	B
43	C
50	D
26	A
41	C
33	D
49	D
27	B
31	B
46	A
34	B
42	C
32	D

38	A
47	C
44	A
48	D
28	B
37	A
36	C
45	D
40	B

5. If you were interested in determining if there was a difference between two groups of students on ranked IQ tests, what test would you use? Assume you have the following data. Do the analysis and write an interpretation.

Group 1	Group 2
1	2
3	6
4	7
5	8
9	10

Chapter 15

Choosing Tests and Writing Interpretations

Orientation _____

   Descriptions of 20 studies follow. The question that each is designed to answer is usually implied rather than stated directly. Most of the studies have been done by students in one of the author's Research Methods course or were inspired by student research ideas. For each description, identify a statistical test that is appropriate for the data.

   Here's a suggestion for getting the most from this exercise. Read each problem, and write down the test to use. Before looking at the answers, turn to Chapter 15 in your textbook. Re-read those sections that deal with choosing the proper statistical test (especially Table 15.1 and Figures 15.1 and 15.2). Using your refreshed knowledge, rework each of the 20 problems. Finally, compare your answers to ours. (Answers to all 20 problems are in the study guide.)

Problems _____

1. Tammy was interested in examining the pattern of visits to the school nurse among 3rd, 4th and 5th grade students in an elementary school. She thought that 3rd graders might be more likely to visit the nurse. She measured the visits for three weeks.

2. Kayla was interested in the examining the development of maturity level from senior year in high school to senior year in college. She used a maturity scale that had been designed and tested at another university. The scale yielded a score from 0 to 100 and reflected the attitudes expressed by the individual. She used a group of seniors from an all male institution and compared that to college men at an all male institution.

3. Shigeru had students on two college campuses fill out surveys on style of dress. From this survey, students could be classified as highly fashion conscious, fashion conscious or not fashion conscious. In addition, he asked students to report their SAT scores.

Chapter 15

4. Lindsay believed that the parenting style displayed by one's primary caregiver was related to success in high school, as measured by class rank.

5. Shari wanted to know if students were more likely to eat breakfast, lunch, or dinner in the college dining hall. For three weeks, she counted the number of students at each meal.

6. Abby and Lilly measured the reaction time of participants who read words as fast as they could from a computer screen. They tested equal numbers of men and women to determine who had faster reaction times. Reaction times are known to be positively skewed.

7. To determine if packages of artificial sweetener all contain the same amount of product (.035 oz), Fran and Ed weighed 30 packages of sweetener.

8. A group of faculty was interested in determining the average incoming SAT scores of student. They had data from the previous 25 years.

9. Chris and Chris had participants read a series of short stories. The stories were inconsistent with previously read material, consistent with previously read material, or unrelated to previously read material. Each participant read 5 stories of each type and reading time was measured.

10. Antonia was studying the behavior of college students on Friday nights. She classified them into one of three groups: studiers, partiers, and sleepers. She then obtained the students' GPAs.

11. Factory workers were asked to report their income. The student interested in this issue wanted to know if this was related to the factory workers' years of service.

12. John and Tracy compared income levels of auto mechanics and car sales people. Income data are known to be positively skewed.

Chapter 15

13. Aubrey examined the influence of course (psychology versus math) and professor's teaching style (lecturer versus discussion based classroom) on test performance.

14. Jane gave students a questionnaire measuring knowledge of statistics. She also asked them to classify whether they took statistics in the math department of the psychology department.

15. Let's assume that women score better on IQ tests than men. How much greater is the IQ score of women than men? Sue has access to IQ scores of more than 2000 men and women.

16. Participants drank both decaffeinated and caffeinated coffee over the course of the morning. After each cup of coffee, participants' reaction time (which is known to be positively skewed) was measured.

17. Participants were given a test of knowledge of US history prior to taking a survey course in history. After finishing the course, they took the test again.

18. Tia wants to know if her major might predict her income when she is 40 years old. She collects data from 100 women who are 40 who had different majors to help her make this prediction.

19. The hearing ability of left-handed and right-handed students was tested by determining the least number of decibels the student could hear.

20. Dave determines his participants' aggression score and then classifies them according to gender and age (either over 40 or under 40).

APPENDIX A

Arithmetic and Algebra Review

Summary _____

This chapter affects different students in different ways. For some, most of the chapter is worthless; these students remember all the arithmetic and algebra perfectly well. For many, it is helpful; students are glad to brush up on a few rusty skills. For a few, it is a most helpful chapter; they never learned the arithmetic and algebra, they don't have the background to continue, and this chapter persuades them to drop the course. If y ou are in the large, middle group, you should mark in your textbook those sections in which you missed problems, find the corresponding section below, and work the problems. For practice in rounding off numbers, work the section in decimals.

Problems _____

Decmials (Round all answers to three decimal places, if rounding is necessary.)

Add:
1. $4.68 + 8 + 2.163 + 1.0005$
2. $185 + .185 + 1.85 + 18.5$
3. $22.06 + 2.534 + .0602 +$
   10.003
4. $5.2 + 12 + 9.74$

Subtract:
5. $456.217 - 82.4$
6. $1.0 - .38751$
7. $89\ 0\ 23.72$
8. $.0456 - .0079$

Multiply:
9. 5.32×2
10. 7.5×8.635
11. $.429 \times .06$
12. $74.62 \times .13$

Divide:
13. $6.82 \div 1.3$
14. $24 \div 2.2$
15. $.356 \div .02$
16. $36.98 \div 74.6$

Fractions

Add:

17. $\dfrac{1}{2} + \dfrac{1}{4} + \dfrac{1}{8}$

18. $\dfrac{2}{3} + \dfrac{3}{4}$

19. $\dfrac{6}{7} + \dfrac{5}{8} + \dfrac{19}{21}$

20. $\dfrac{4}{5} + \dfrac{2}{3}$

Subtract:

21. $\dfrac{3}{8} - \dfrac{1}{5}$

22. $\dfrac{16}{23} - \dfrac{11}{13}$

23. $\dfrac{1}{5} - \dfrac{1}{8}$

24. $\dfrac{2}{3} - \dfrac{8}{9}$

Multiply:

25. $\dfrac{2}{3} \times \dfrac{4}{7}$

26. $\dfrac{4}{5} \times \dfrac{1}{3}$

27. $\dfrac{7}{10} \times \dfrac{1}{2} \times \dfrac{2}{3}$

28. $\dfrac{3}{4} \times \dfrac{1}{3} \times \dfrac{3}{8}$

Divide:

29. $\dfrac{1}{2} \div \dfrac{1}{3}$

30. $\dfrac{3}{4} \div \dfrac{1}{2}$

31. $\dfrac{12}{19} \div \dfrac{6}{7}$

32. $25 \div \dfrac{1}{2}$

Appendix A

Negative Numbers

Add:
33. $(-2) + (3)$
34. $(-28) + (-12)$
35. $(-16) + (-3) + (-15) + (-21)$
36. $(-8) + (-5) + (35)$

Multiply:
41. $(-5) \times (-2)$
42. $(4) \times (-6)$
43. $(-10) \times (-14)$
44. $(-21) \times (7)$

Subtract:
37. $(-8) - (-5)$
38. $(16) - (-12)$
39. $(-23) - (-21)$
40. $(263) - (-158)$

Divide:
45. $(-4) \div (-2)$
46. $(8) \div (-3)$
47. $(-26) \div (12)$
48. $(-15) \div (-21)$

Percents and proportions

49. A class is made up of 12 males and 15 females. What proportion is female?
50. The same class has 10 left-handed students and 17 right-handed students. What percent is left-handed?
51. If 22% of the students in the class of 27 are left-handed females, how many are there?
52. How many left-handed males are in the class?

Absolute value

53. $6 + |-5|$
54. $|7| + (-3)$
55. $|-8| - |-6|$
56. $10 \times |-4|$

± Problems

57. 10 ± 18
58. 52 ± 6.5
59. -8 ± 3.25
60. $.32 \pm .35$

146

Appendix A

Exponents

61. 6^2
62. 2.38^2
63. 18.5^2
64. $.009^2$

Complex Problems _____

(Round all answers to three decimal places.)

65. $\dfrac{8+1+4+6}{3}$

66. $\dfrac{(10-6-5+2)^2 + (6-3-4+4)^2}{4(5+3)}$

67. $\dfrac{\left(66 - \dfrac{12^2}{10}\right) + \left(75 - \dfrac{8^2}{5}\right)}{10-1}$

68. $\dfrac{(5)(20)-(15)(6)}{\sqrt{[(5)(38)-(150)][(5)(22)-(193)]}}$

69. $\dfrac{\dfrac{225}{9} - (12)(6)}{(8.5)(6.3)}$

70. $36 - (1.96)\left(\dfrac{2}{\sqrt{100}}\right)$

71. $\dfrac{5.6 - 12.4}{\sqrt{\left(\dfrac{32+41}{5+6-2}\right)\left(\dfrac{1}{6}+\dfrac{1}{3}\right)}}$

72. $\sqrt{\dfrac{21-\dfrac{(-8)^2}{6}}{6}}$

73. $\sqrt{\dfrac{\left[68-\dfrac{(5)^2}{2}+54-\dfrac{(11)^2}{5}\right]}{6(8-1)}}$

74. $\dfrac{\left(\dfrac{112}{8}-\dfrac{73+84}{8+8}\right)^2}{\dfrac{13.26}{8}+\dfrac{13.26}{8+8}}$

Simple Algebra (Solve for x.)

75. $\dfrac{x+5}{3}=4.25$

76. $\dfrac{24-4}{x}=6.42$

77. $\dfrac{15-7}{4}=2x-2$

78. $\dfrac{12-3}{3}=\dfrac{3x+5}{2}$

APPENDIX B

Grouped Frequency Distributions
and Central Tendency

Summary _____

Compiling a large set of unorganized scores into a *grouped frequency distribution* makes understanding the scores much easier. A grouped frequency distribution consists of *class intervals* and *frequencies* and can be presented as a table, a graph, or both. Each class interval covers the same number of scores (which is *not* the number of frequencies). The number of scores in an interval is symbolized *i*.

There are four conventions for creating class intervals:
1. the number of class intervals should be 10 to 20.
2. the size of *I* should be odd (unless you use *I* = 2, or 10, or a multiple of 10)
3. the lower limit of each class interval should be a multiple of *i*. (But when *i* = 4, the midpoint of the interval should be a multiple of 5.)
4. the higher scores go at the top of the table.

To find the mean of a grouped frequency distribution, multiply each class-interval midpoint by the frequency in the interval. Sum these products, and divide by *N* (which is the sum of the *f* column).

To find the median, use the formula $\dfrac{N+1}{2}$ to locate the middle frequency. Add frequencies from the bottom of the distribution until you locate the class interval that contains the number produced by the formula above. The midpoint of that interval is the median.

The mode is the midpoint of the class interval that occurs with the greatest frequency.

Appendix B

Problems_____

1. The general result of damage to the left cerebrum of a right-handed person is a lower IQ (Presumably this is due to reduced ability in logical, convergent thinking – a left brain function.). Jeanette McGlone asked if this conclusion was true for both men and women. (This is a fairly typical example of extending knowledge – finding out if what is true for a population is also true for each subgroup.) The numbers below are IQ scores for left-brain damaged, right handed females. The mean of these numbers is the same as that found by McGlone. Group these data into an appropriate frequency distribution, draw a graph, and find any measures of central tendency that are appropriate. Write a sentence of interpretation about the mean.

78	119	94	88	113	126	103	81	100	103
103	98	105	90	74	101	89	96	85	100
96	100	88	111	98	93	121	110	113	79
99									

2. A class of college students was asked to list all the states in the USA. The numbers they produced are shown below. Arrange them into an appropriate frequency distribution and from the distribution, find the mean, median and mode.

18	34	25	32	18	40	12	38	26	40	23	29	38
23	26	42	21	9	35	25	17	15	25	37	24	12
45	28	13	22	16	28	32	25	41	27	19	24	18
16	46	28	39	11	25	45	20	29	33	21		

3. Arrange each set of scores into a grouped frequency distribution. The median of each distribution is gen in the answer (in case you need additional practice in finding the median).
    a.

50	40	55	57	59	42	44	44
39	36	42	31	52	50	40	43
39	35	61	57	49	57	60	67
51	50	40	37	42	52	62	50

150

Appendix B

b.

```
29  39  49  27  37  47  52  39  17  18
21  60  42  51  12  19  29  42  61  4
8   27  68  38  17  0   17  14  0   3
47  48  29  21  17
```

4. Arrange the scores into a grouped frequency distribution and find the mean and the median.

```
38  22  27  41  37  13  33  35  31  36  36  32  15
31  40  35  34  24  36  30  18  25  37  27  30  34
35  38  37  28  34  19  37  32  29  33  21  26  31
38
```

ANSWERS TO ODD-NUMBERED PROBLEMS

CHAPTER 1

Multiple-Choice Questions _____
1. 2   3. 1   5. 4   7. 3   9. 3
11. 1   13. 4   15. 1   17. 2   19. 1

Short-Answer Questions _____
1.
    a. A descriptive statistic is an index number that is in some way characteristic of or informative about a large group of numbers. Inferential statistics is a method of drawing conclusions about populations from samples taken from populations.
    b. A population contains all of the scores that exist for a given group. A sample is a subset of scores drawn from that group.
    c. Different numbers on an *interval scale* have the following relationships: different numbers stand for different things (or amounts); larger numbers mean more of the thing than smaller numbers; and the differences between numbers on the scale are all the same. *Ordinal scales* have only the first and second characteristics named here.

Problems _____
1A.   a. room color
    b. 3; red, blue, and white
    c. mood survey scores
    d. all worked the same logic problems, amount of time in the room
    e. room color
    f. mood survey; ordinal
    g. The mood of participants working difficult problems was affected by the color of the room. A red room led to participants being more agitated than working in a white room. Participants working in a blue room reported being calmest of all.

1B.   a. parenting style
    b. 3; authoritarian, authoritative, permissive

c. GPA
d. age of the participants
e. parenting style
f. GPA; interval is a good answer; ordinal is acceptable
g. Khiela's study did not show that parenting style has an effect on college grade point average.

3. What are the lower and upper limits of the following numbers?
    a. 1.25 – 1.35
    b. 7.5 – 8.5
    c. 22.5-23.5°F
    d. $45.495 - $45.505
    e. 9.995-10.005 grams

5. Identify the kind of scale that each set of values comes from.
    a. nominal
    b. nominal
    c. ratio
    d. interval
    e. nominal
    f. ordinal
    g. ratio

7. Identify each measurement below as being based on a quantitative or qualitative variable. For quantitative variables identify the lower and upper limits of the measurement.
    a. Quantitative: 413.5-414.5
    b. Quantitative: 15.5 – 16.5
    c. Qualitative
    d. Quantitative: 2.95-3.05
    e. Quantitative: 101.85-101.95
    f. Quantitative: 23.945-23.955
    g. Quantitative: 4 minutes, 14.5 seconds - 4 minutes, 15.5 seconds
    h. Quantitative: 0.865-0.875

9. The independent variable is deprivation with levels of thirst, hunger and sex. The dependent variable is the amount of electrical shock the rat tolerated. Age, gender, and experience of the rat should have been controlled (Other answers can be correct here.)

CHAPTER 2

Multiple Choice _____

1. 4   3. 4   5. 4   7. 3   9. 1
11. 4   13. 2   15. 4

Short-Answer Questions _____

1. A frequency polygon consists of dots connected by lines and is used to present one or more sets of quantitative data. A histogram, which consists of touching bars, is used to present one set of quantitative data. A bar graph has space between the bars and is used to present qualitative data. A line graph shows the relationship between two variables.

Problems _____

1.   a.

X	f
11	1
10	3
9	6
Σ	10

This distribution is positively skewed.

b.

X	f
6	1
5	4
4	2
3	1
2	4
1	1
Σ	13

This distribution is bimodal.

3.

X	f
4	6
3	3
2	5
1	3
0	23
Σ	40

Most people drive to work. The distribution is positively skewed.

5.

GRE scores	
Class Interval	f
237-245	1
228-236	1
219-227	0
210-218	2
201-209	0
192-200	2
183-191	3
174-182	5
165-173	6
156-164	4
147-155	4
138-146	1
129-137	3
120-128	2
111-119	1
	$\Sigma = 35$

Chapter 3

Multiple-Choice Questions _____

1. 3   3. 2   5. 2   7. 1   9. 3
11. 3   13. 3   15. 3   17. 3   19. 1

Short-Answer Questions _____

1. The median should be used if a class interval is open ended, the observations are nominal or ordinal data, or if the distribution is severely skewed.

3. The median would be smaller. The mean is pulled toward the higher scores when a distribution is skewed, as this one is. The median, unaffected by skewness, remains in the center of the distribution.

5. σ is the standard deviation of a population. $\hat{s}$ is used to estimate a population standard deviation from a sample and S is used to describe the variability of a sample of data when you have no intention of drawing inferences about the larger population.

Problems _____

1. Did you estimate a central tendency value before you began the problem? "About 6" is a good estimate.

X	f
6.2	1
6.1	2
5.9	1
5.8	1
Σ	3495

Mean = $\bar{X} = \dfrac{30.1}{5} = 6.02$. Median location = $\dfrac{N+1}{2} = \dfrac{5}{2} = 2.5$. The median is among the two 6.1's. The median is 6.1. The mode is 6.1.

Bonus answer: Avogadro claims 6.02 as his number. (In 1811, the Italian physicist, Avogadro (1776-1856) hypothesized that equal volumes of gas under equal conditions contain equal numbers of molecules. We now know that under a standard condition, that number is 6.02×10^{23}, a quantity referred to as Avogadro's number.)

3. College students: mean = 3.75, median = 4, mode = 4, 5
   Older adults: mean = 2.27, median = 2, mode = 1

5. Men: Range: 244-112=132 pounds

Interquartile range: $N = 35$. Thus, .25 x 35 = 8.75. Counting from the top of the distribution to find the 75th percentile, you find 6 frequencies above the interval 183-191 pounds (which has 3 frequencies). The 75th percentile is the midpoint of the interval, 187 pounds. Counting from the bottom of the distribution for the 25th percentile, you find 7 frequencies below the interval

of 147-155 pounds (which has 4 frequencies). The 25th percentile is 151, the midpoint of the interval.
IQR = 187-151 = 36 pounds.

Women: Range: 218-95= 123 pounds

Interquartile range: N = 35. Thus, .25 x 35 = 8.75. Counting from the top of the distribution to find the 75th percentile, you find 6 frequencies above the interval 154-162 pounds. The 75th percentile is the midpoint of the interval, 158 pounds. The 8.75th score from the bottom is among the 6 in the interval, 118-126 pounds. The 25th percentile is 122. IQR = 158-122 = 36 pounds.

7.

X	f	X-$\bar{X}$	$(X$-$\bar{X})^2$	$f(X$-$\bar{X})^2$
9	1	2	4	4
8	2	1	1	2
7	6	0	0	0
6	2	-1	1	2
5	1	-2	4	4
	Σ=15	0		12

$$\sigma = \sqrt{\frac{\sum f(X-\bar{X})^2}{N}} = \sqrt{\frac{12}{12}} = 1.00 \text{ digit;}$$

Range = 9-5 = 4; IQR = 8 – 6 = 2 digits.

9.

X	X^2
17	289
14	196
11	121
10	100
8	64
Σ = 60	770

158

$$\bar{X} = 12.00$$
$$\Sigma X = 60$$
$$\Sigma X^2 = 770$$

$$\sigma = \sqrt{\frac{770 - \frac{60^2}{5}}{5}} = 3.16$$

$$\sigma^2 = 10$$

Chapter 4

Multiple choice_____

1. 3   3. 3   5. 2   7. 1   9. 3
11. 3   13. 4   15. 4   17. 1   19. 4

Short-Answer Questions _____

1. A z of 0 is the z score for the mean in a distribution of raw scores.

3. A boxplot shows the mean, median, range and interquartile range. By comparing the positions of the mena and median and by comparing the length of the whiskers, you can determine if the distribution is symmetrical or skewed and the direction of skew.

Problems _____

1.

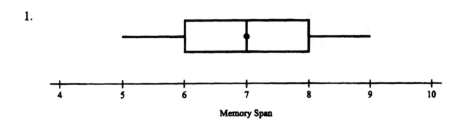

Memory Span

The average number of digits a person can hear and repeat without error is symmetrically distributed about 7. The range is 5 to 9 digits; the IQR is 2 digits; σ is1.00. (A common way to summarize this universal finding is that human memory span is 7 ± 2 chunks. A digit is an example of a chunk.)

3.

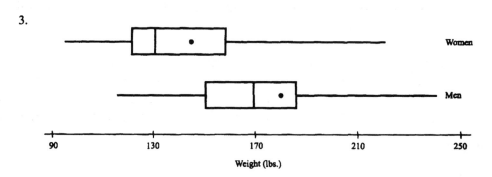

Weights are positively skewed; for men ages 20-29, mean weight is 180 pounds, the median is 169 pounds. For women of the same age, the mean is 145 pounds, the median is 131 pounds. Men weigh more than women; the effect size is 0.88, a value that is considered large. There is, however, some overlap among the middle 50 percent of each population.

5. $d = 0.10$ is a small effect size, suggesting that the difference in cognitive ability between first born children and second born children is not substantial.

7. a. 92   b. 121   c. 141   d. 71

Chapter 5

Multiple-Choice Questions _____

1. 3   3. 1   5. 3   7. 3   9. 4
11. 1   13. 4   15. 2   17. 2   19. 4

Short-Answer Questions _____

1. The more self-confidence a recruit has, the less likely he or she will be successful.

3. There is some tendency for students scoring higher on the LSAT to earn better grades in the first year of law school than students with relatively low LSAT scores. This tendency, however, is not very strong. The LSAT accounts for only 13% of the variance in grades ($r^2 = .13$) with the other 87% unaccounted for.

Part of the reason for this low correlation is due to truncation of range. In these data, the correlation is computed only on students selected for law school, nearly all of whom had high scores on the LSAT. The range of scores (variability in the scores) is thus restricted. In like manner, grade distributions in law school tend to be restricted to higher grades (mostly A and B). Such restrictions on variability always reduces the size of r.

5. a. The correlation coefficient is based on an N of 100. Each of the 100 items have both a mean score from the nuns and from the child molesters.
b. Nuns and child molesters have the same ideas about social desirability. They agree about what is desirable and what is not.

Problems _____

1.
$$\bar{X} = \frac{3500}{50} = 70.00$$

$$\bar{Y} = \frac{115}{50} = 2.30$$

$$S_x = \sqrt{\frac{250,000 - \frac{3500^2}{50}}{50}} = 10.00$$

$$S_y = \sqrt{\frac{289 - \frac{115^2}{50}}{50}} = 0.70$$

a. $r = \dfrac{\dfrac{8084}{50} - (70)(2.30)}{10(.70)} = .097$

$r = \dfrac{(50)(8084) - (3500)(115)}{\sqrt{[(50)(250,000) - 3500^2][50(289) - 115^2]}} = .097$

b. $b = (.097)\dfrac{.70}{10} = 0.0068$

$a = 2.30 - (0.0068)(70) = 1.825$

$Y' = 1.825 + 0.0068X$

c. $Y' = 1.825 + (0.0068)(100) = 2.51$

d. Because the degree of relationship between sensory ability and GPA is so slight (the r is only .09), not much faith can be put in any regression equation prediction. That is, a wide range of GPA's around 2.51 would be expected for those students whose sensory score was 100.

3.

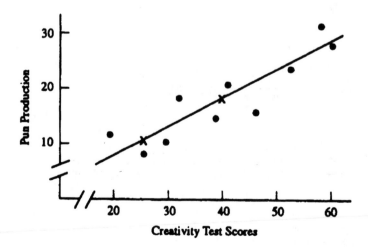

Student	X	Y	X^2	Y^2	XY
1	60	28	3600	784	1680
2	57	32	3249	1024	1824
3	52	24	2704	576	1248
4	46	16	2116	256	736
5	41	21	1681	441	861
6	38	14	1444	196	532
7	32	18	1024	324	576
8	29	11	841	121	319
9	25	9	625	81	225
10	19	12	361	144	228
$\Sigma=$	399	18	17,64	3947	8229

$$\overline{X} = \frac{399}{10} = 39.9 \qquad \overline{Y} = \frac{185}{10} = 18.5$$

$$S_X = \sqrt{\frac{17.645 - \dfrac{399^2}{10}}{10}} \qquad S_Y = \sqrt{\frac{3947 - \dfrac{185^2}{10}}{10}}$$

$$= 13.1335 \qquad\qquad\qquad = 7.2422$$

$$r = \frac{\dfrac{8229}{10} - (39.9)(18.5)}{(13.1335)(7.24422)} = \frac{84.75}{95.1154} = .89$$

$$r = \frac{(10)(82298) - (399)(185)}{\sqrt{[(10)(17,645) - (399^2)][(10)(3947) - (185^2)]}}$$

$$= \frac{8475}{\sqrt{(17,249)(5245)}} = \frac{8475}{9511.6247} = .89$$

163

$$r^2 = (.89)^2 = .79$$

$$b = (.89) \frac{7.2422}{13.1335} = 0.49$$

$$a = 18.5 - (.49)(39.9) = -1.05$$

$$\hat{Y} = -1.05 + .49X$$

$$\hat{Y} = -1.05 + .49(25) = 11.2$$

The scatterplot shows that the relationship between creativity test scores and the production of puns is linear. The correlation coefficient is quite high with $r = .89$. With a coefficient of determination of $.79$, you can say that almost 80 percent of the variance of the two tests is common variance. The two tests seem to be tapping the same abilities. In sum, data such as these support the hypothesis that there is a relationship between creativity and humor.

5.

Student	X	Y	X^2	Y^2	XY
1	28	3.16	784	9.99	88.48
2	4	2.55	16	6.5	10.20
3	47	3.10	2209	9.61	145.7
4	19	3.97	361	15.76	75.43
5	43	1.84	1849	3.39	79.12
6	50	2.99	2500	8.94	149.50
7	34	2.07	1156	4.28	70.38
8	21	3.01	441	9.06	63.21
$\Sigma =$	246	22.69	9316	67.53	682.02

$$\bar{X} = \frac{246}{8} = 30.75 \qquad\qquad \bar{Y} = \frac{22.69}{8} = 2.84$$

$$S_x = \sqrt{\dfrac{9316 - \dfrac{246^2}{8}}{8}} = 14.80 \qquad S_y = \sqrt{\dfrac{67.53 - \dfrac{22.69^2}{8}}{8}} = 0.63$$

$$r = \dfrac{\dfrac{682.02}{8} - (30.75)(2.84)}{(14.80)(0.63)} = -0.22$$

$$b = (-0.22)\dfrac{0.63}{14.80} = -0.0094$$

$$a = 2.84 - (-0.0094)(30.75) = 3.13$$

$$Y' = 3.13 + (-0.0094)X$$

$$Y' = 3.13 + (-0.0094)4 = 3.09$$

Thus, a student with a class rank of 4 would have a GPA predicted to be 3.09.

Chapter 6

Multiple-Choice Questions _____

1. 3   3. 4   5. 3   7. 4   9. 3
11. 1   13. 3   15. 3   17. 3   19. 1

Short-Answer Questions _____

1. A theoretical distribution is based on mathematics and logic, whereas an empirical distribution is obtained from observations.

3. The total number of students is 1400.

    a. $\dfrac{500}{1400} = .36$

    b. $\dfrac{200}{1400} = .14$

c. $\dfrac{400 = 300}{1400} = .50$

d. Subtracting answer (b) (.14) from 1.00 gives .86.

5. The binomial distribution is based on the probability of event occurring that have only two possible outcomes. Normal distributions are based on events that have multiple outcomes.

Problems _____

1. a. empirical   d. empirical
   b. empirical   e. empirical
   c. empirical   f. empirical

3.

a. $z = \dfrac{23 - 20}{4} = 0.75, p = .2266$

b. $z = \dfrac{27 - 20}{4} = 1.75, p = .0401$

c. $z = \dfrac{36 - 20}{4} = 4.00, p = .00003$

The probability of obtaining 36 matches in 100 attempts by chance alone is .00003. Some other explanation (like ESP or cheating) seems more likely.

5.   a. $z = \dfrac{1 - 7}{3.74} = = -1.60$, proportion $= .0548$

b. Figure 5.1 shows a proportion of .077

c. The distribution of playing cards is rectangular but the normal curve was used to calculate the proportion .0548.

7. a. For $z = 2.00$, proportion $= .0228$; $.0228 \times 1000 = 22.8$ or about 23 people. Normal curve with scores and proportions needed for Problems 7b, 7c, and 7d.

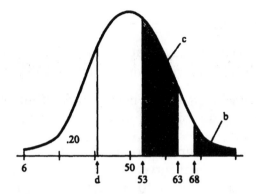

d. $z = \dfrac{68 - 50}{10} = 1.80$, proportion = .0359

e. $z = \dfrac{63 - 50}{10} = 1.30$, proportion = .4232 and $z = \dfrac{53 - 50}{10} = 0.30$,

proportion = 0.1179; .4302 – 0.1179 = .2853, the proportion scoring between 53 and 63.

f. The z score associated with a proportion of .20 that is below the mean is -.84.

$-.84 = \dfrac{X - 50}{10} = 41.6$, the score that separates out the lowest one-fifth of the population

Chapter 7

Multiple-Choice Questions _____

1. 2   3. 2   5. 2   7. 3   9. 3
11. 1   13. 3   15. 1   17. 2   19. 3

Short-Answer Questions _____

1. The Central Limit Theorem says that the form of the sampling distribution of the mean of any population will have a mean equal to μ, a standard deviation equal to $\dfrac{\sigma}{\sqrt{N}}$, and will approach a normal curve if sample size is large.

3. According to the Central Limit Theorem, the sampling distribution of the mean will approach a normal curve, regardless of the shape of the population distribution, if the sample size is 30 or greater. The techniques of Chapter 7 are, therefore, appropriate for this skewed distribution when the sample size is this large.

5. The confidence interval can tell us that we have 95% confidence that a particular range contains the population mean. If our sample mean is outside of that range, it is probably not from that distribution.

Problems _____

1. $\sigma_{\bar{x}} = \dfrac{100}{\sqrt{50}} = 14.14$

    $z = \dfrac{\bar{X} - \mu}{\sigma_{\bar{x}}} = \dfrac{725 - 750}{14.14} = -1.77$

    $p = .0384$

    The claim is on somewhat shaky ground. If the claim of 750 hours is correct, you would expect to get a mean of 725 or lower from 50 bulbs less than 4% of the time.

3. $\bar{X} = \dfrac{11.340}{36} = 315;$ $\quad = 60.00;\ s_{\bar{x}} = \dfrac{60}{\sqrt{36}} = 10$

    $t_{99}(30\ df) = 2.75$

    $LL = \bar{X} - t(s_{\bar{x}}) = 315 - 2.75(10.00) = 287.5$ volts

    $UL = \bar{X} + t(s_{\bar{x}}) = 315 + 2.75(10.00) = 342.5$ volts

The mean shock level of the students at the college with humanitarian ideals is between 287.5 volts and 342.5 volts (99 percent confidence). Because the mean value for Americans is 285 volts, conclude that the students at the College of HI are willing to administer more shock (be more cruel, perhaps) than the average American.

5. $\bar{X} = \dfrac{1224}{36} = 34.001;$ $= 2.402;$ $\dfrac{725 - 750}{14.14} = -1.77 = 0.400$

$t_{95}(30 \text{ } df) = 2.042$

LL $= 34.00 - 2.042(0.400) = 33.18$

UL $= 34.00 + 2.042(0.400) = 34.82$

We are 95 percent confident that the interval 33.18 to 34.82 contains the unknown population mean of the film. Because the interval is entirely above 33, the population mean of all films, conclude that the students rated this film higher than the average film.

7. Each person's sample is likely to be different. What is important is the procedure.
   a. Identify each score with a one-digit number from 0 to 9.
   b. Haphazardly find a place to start in the table of random numbers.
   c. Record the first six digits you come to, ignoring a digit that appears more than once.
   d. Translate the six digits into the six scores, which now constitute a random sample.

Chapter 8

Multiple-Choice Questions _____

1. 2   3. 1   5. 3   7. 3   9. 3
11. 4   13. 4   15. 4   17. 2   19. 2

Short-Answer Questions _____

  1. A Type I error is committed when you conclude that the null hypothesis is false but it is, in fact, true. A Type II error is committed when you do not reject a false null hypothesis.

  3. A null hypothesis is rejected when the difference between the sample statistic and the population parameter is so large that the difference is unlikely, *if the null hypothesis is true.* The null hypothesis is retained when the difference between the sample statistic and the population parameter is not very large; that is, the difference is what you would expect if the null hypothesis is true. When you reject the null hypothesis, you are left with an alternative hypothesis. When you retain the null hypothesis, you are left with it *and* the alternative hypothesis.

  5. a. H_0: $\mu_0 = 285$. $t_{.05}$ (19 *df*) = 2.093. Retain the null hypothesis. There isn't a statistically significant difference willingness to provide "shock" now versus in the early 1960's
  b. $r_{.05}$ (20 *df*) = .4227. (From Table A, Appendix B.). A correlation coefficient of .44 is statistically significant. We could conclude that there is strong agreement of what facial expressions represent across cultures.

Problems _____

1. $\Sigma X = 540$ $\qquad\qquad$ $\Sigma X^2 = 25{,}036$
  $\overline{X} = 45.00;$ $\quad = 8.180;$ $s_{\overline{x}} = 2.361$
  $t = \dfrac{45.51}{2.361} = -2.54;$ *df* = 11
  $t_{.05}$ (11 *df*) = 2.201

Students who were in academic difficulty had a mean Personal Control Score that was less than the norm for college students (p < .05).

$$d = \frac{45.51}{8.18} = -0.734$$

The effect size index 0.73 indicates that being in academic difficulty has an effect on PC scores that is classified as large (almost).

3. $\bar{X} = \frac{235}{30} = 7.83;$ $= \sqrt{\frac{1931 - \frac{235^2}{30}}{29}} = 1.763;$ $s_{\bar{x}} \frac{1.763}{\sqrt{30}} = 0.322$

$t = \frac{7.83 - 7}{0.322} = 2.578;$ df = 29 $\qquad d = \frac{7.83 - 7}{1.763} = .47$

$t_{.05}$ (29 df) = 2.045. Since our obtained t value exceed the critical t value, we can claim we have a group that has shown significant improvement in short term memory capacity (we can reject our null hypothesis). The effect size (d = 0.44) is a medium effect size estimate.

5. $\Sigma X = 200$ $\qquad\qquad \Sigma X^2 = 1206$
$\bar{X} = 5;$ $\quad = 2.30;$ $s_{\bar{x}} = .364$

$t = \frac{5 - 6}{.34} = -2.75;$ df = 39 $\qquad d = \frac{5 - 6}{2.30} = .43$

$t_{.05}$ (30 df) = 2.042. There is a significance difference between what participants typically choose in this situation versus what they do when exposed to low numbers. The effect size, d=.43, suggesting that this is a medium effect.

Overall interpretation: Direct, blatant stimuli are more effective in changing behavior than subtle, subliminal stimuli.

Chapter 9

Multiple-Choice Questions _____

1. 4   3. 2   5. 3   7. 2   9. 3
11. 4   13. 4   15. 4   17. 4   19. 4

Short-Answer Questions _____

1.
- a. Paired samples; $df = 13$
- b. Paired samples; $df = 20$
- c. Independent samples; $df = 28$
- d. Independent samples; $df = 22$
- e. Paired samples; $df = 33$

3. a. Actual difference between the populations. The greater the actual difference, the
   more likely the rejection of the null hypothesis.
   b. The size of the standard error of a difference. The smaller it is, the more
   likely the rejection of the null hypothesis. It can be made smaller by
   increasing sample size or reducing sample variability.
   c. Alpha. The larger alpha is, the more likely the rejection of the null
   hypothesis.

5. a. The populations the samples are from are normally distributed.
   b. The populations the samples are from have variances that are equal.
   c. Extraneous variables are eliminated, perhaps by random assignment of
   participants to groups.

7. If you worked the problems yourself, you probably were stumped for a while on
   No. 8. The method (set) you had developed by solving the first seven did not
   work for the eighth. How adaptable were you? Did you abandon your set quickly
   when it did not work, or did you stick with it?

   This is an independent-samples design. The first seven problems established
   a mental set that solved the problem. That set was "fill the middle jar and from it

fill the left jar once and the right jar twice." This set was detrimental in solving the eighth problem, which could be easily solved by "fill the left jar and from it fill the right jar once."

9. When using a pre-post test measure, the best statistical procedure to use is the paired samples t test..

Problems _____

1.

Participant	Before	After	D	D^2
1	5	6	-1	1
2	4	4	0	0
3	3	5	-2	4
4	3	4	-1	1
5	2	4	-2	4
6	2	3	-1	1
7	1	3	-2	4
8	0	2	-2	4
	$\Sigma = 20$	31	-11	19

$$\overline{X} = 2.50$$

$$s_D = \sqrt{\frac{19 - \dfrac{-11^2}{8}}{7}} = \sqrt{\frac{19 - 15.1250}{7}} = \sqrt{\frac{3.8750}{7}} = \sqrt{.5336} = .7440$$

$$s_{\overline{D}} = .\frac{.7440}{\sqrt{8}} = .2630$$

$$t = \frac{2.50 - 3.875}{.2630} = 5.228;$$

$$df = N - 1 = 8 - 1 = 7 \quad t_{.01}(7 \; df) = 3.499 \qquad p < .01$$

$$d = \frac{\overline{X}_1 - \overline{X}_2}{s_D} = \frac{1.375}{.7440} = 1.848$$

The boys displayed significantly more hostility toward minority groups after frustration than they did before. The effect size index, 1.85, shows that the effect of frustration is quite large. Note that this is purely a psychological effect - the minority groups were not actually present in the experiment and not connected with the frustration.

3.

	Shown	Not Shown
ΣX	80	118
ΣX^2	1120	2392
N	6	6
$\bar{X}$	13.333	19.667
	3.2660	3.771

$$\hat{s}_{\bar{x}1} = \frac{3.2660}{\sqrt{6}} = 1.333 \qquad \hat{s}_{\bar{x}2} = \frac{3.7771}{\sqrt{6}} = 1.5420$$

$$s_{\bar{x}1-\bar{x}2} = \sqrt{1.3333^2 + 1.5420^2} = \sqrt{1.7777 + 2.3778} = 2.0385$$

$t_{.95}(10 \ df) = 2.228$

$LL = (\bar{X}_1 - \bar{X}_2) - t(s \ \bar{X}_1 - \bar{X}_2) = (19.667 - 13.333) - 2.228(2.0385) = 1.79$ seconds

$UL = (\bar{X}_1 - \bar{X}_2) + t(s \bar{X}_1 - \bar{X}_2) = (19.667 - 13.333) + 2.228(2.0385) = 10.88$ seconds

We can be 95 percent confident that the effect of watching other cats solve the problem reduces the time needed to solve the problem by 1.79 to 10.88 seconds. That is, cats learn by imitation; the data support Hobhouse. (Indeed, this experiment was modeled after one by Hobhouse.) [Note that because 0 is not in the 95 percent confidence interval, the null hypothesis can be rejected at the .05 level.]

5. We would use an independent samples t since the people are in separate groups.

	Changed answers	Did not change answers
ΣX	413	378
ΣX^2	43,685	28,786
N	5	5

$$\overline{X} \qquad 82.6 \qquad 75.60$$
$$\qquad\qquad 11.94 \qquad 7.23$$

$$\hat{s}_{\overline{x}1} = \frac{11.94}{\sqrt{5}} = 5.34 \qquad\qquad \hat{s}_{\overline{x}2} = \frac{7.23}{\sqrt{5}} = 3.23$$

$$s_{\overline{x}1-\overline{x}2} = \sqrt{s\overline{x}_1^{\,2} + s\overline{x}_2^{\,2}} = \sqrt{5.34^2 + 3.23^2} = \sqrt{28.52 + 10.43} = 6.24$$

$$t = \frac{\overline{X}_1 - \overline{X}_2}{s_{\overline{x}1-\overline{x}2}} = \frac{82.6 - 75.60}{6.24} = 1.12$$

$t_{(.05)} (8\ df) = 2.306$

Since our obtained t value does not exceed the critical value, we retain the null hypothesis and conclude that there is no evidence to support the idea that there is a difference in scores on exams based on whether or not a participant changes his or her answers. From a purely theoretical standpoint, however, this experiment has perhaps too few participants, and thus low power, to reject a null, given the null was false.

Chapter 10

Multiple-Choice Questions _____

1. 4   3. 3   5. 3   7. 3   9. 2
11. 2   13. 3   15. 2   17. 2   19. 4

Interpretation _____

1. The independent variable is hospital location (Crimea, England, France) or hospital type (military, civilian). The dependent variable is "improvement scores." The F value produced by the ratio of the two mean squares is 6.04. Because $F_{.01}$ (2,32 df) = 5.34, you can conclude that there are significant differences among the hospital populations in improvement scores.

The f value is 0.529, which is large. The effect of the hospital location has a large effect on improvement scores.

The $s_{\bar{x}}$ = value for Tukey tests is 1.31. The tabled value for HSD at the .01 level for three groups and a df_{error} of 32 is 4.46. When England and Crimea are compared HSD = 4.58. (The value for the France-Crimea comparison is even larger). A comparison of England and France produces an HSD of 0.76. Patients in the military hospital in Crimea showed significantly greater improvement scores than patients in either English or French hospitals. The English and French hospitals were not significantly different.

3. The ANOVA method described in Chapter 10 requires independent groups. These
   data are correlated because each wine taster rated all four wines. A correlated measures design is required for this problem. (See Chapter 12.)

5. The ANOVA is a statistical procedure that works to compare two or more means. If there are only two means, you can use either a t test or an ANOVA. Both will yield similar results that will allow for the same type of interpretation.

Problems _____

1. Independent variable: Predictability of reinforcement
   Dependent variable: Persistence during extinction

	Very Predictable	Fairly Predictable	Unpredictable
	8	16	18
	13	11	19
	11	15	22
	8		16
			15
ΣX	40	42	90
ΣX^2	418	602	1650
$\bar{X}$	10	14	18

$$SS_{tot} = 2670 - \frac{172^2}{12} = 204.67$$

$$SS_{treat} = \frac{40^2}{4} + \frac{42^2}{3} + \frac{90^2}{5} - \frac{172^2}{12} = 142.67$$

$$SS_{error} = [418 - \frac{40^2}{4}] + [602 - \frac{42^2}{3}] + [1650 - \frac{90^2}{5}] = 62.00$$

CHECK: $142.67 + 62.00 = 204.67$

Source	SS	df	MS	F
Predictability	142.67	2	71.335	10.35
Error	62.00	9	6.888	
Total	204.67	11		

$F_{.01}$ (2,9 df) = 8.02. The three schedules produced significantly different amounts of persistence during extinction. Three Tukey HSD tests produce

HSD (Very vs. Fairly) = 2.84

HSD (Fairly vs. Un) = 2.96

HSD (Very vs. Un) = 6.45

$HSD_{.01}$ = 5.43. Persistence during extinction depends on the predictability of reinforcement during learning. Unpredictable reinforcement leads to significantly more persistence than very predictable reinforcement.

3. $\Sigma X_{tot} = 49 + 74 + 78 + 83 = 284$
   $\Sigma X^2{}_{tot} = 269 + 574 + 636 + 711 = 2190$

$$SS_{tot} = 2190 - \frac{284^2}{40} = 173.60$$

$$SS_{anesthetics} = \frac{49^2}{10} + \frac{74^2}{10} + \frac{78^2}{10} + \frac{83^2}{10} - \frac{284^2}{40} = 68.60$$

$$SS_{error} = [\,269 - \frac{49^2}{10}\,] + [\,574 - \frac{74^2}{10}\,] + [\,636 - \frac{78^2}{10}\,] + [\,\frac{711 - 83^2}{10}\,]$$
$$= 28.90 + 26.40 + 27.60 + 22.10 = 105$$

CHECK: $173.60 = 68.60 + 105$

Source	SS	df	MS	F	p
Anesthetics	68.60	3	22.8667	7.84	< .01
Error	105.00	36	2.9167		
Total	173.60	39			

$$f = \frac{\sqrt{\frac{3}{40}(22.8667 - 2.9167)}}{\sqrt{2.9167}} = 0.716$$

An $f = 0.716$ is larger than 0.40, a value that is considered large. Thus, anesthetics have a large effect on Apgar scores.

The $s_{\bar{x}}$ required for Tukey HSD tests is

$$\sqrt{\frac{2.9176}{10}} = .540 \qquad\qquad HSD_{.05} = 3.84$$

When the HSD tests are calculated, the Apgar scores of twilight neonates is significantly lower than any of other three methods. The other three methods do not differ significantly among themselves.

5.   Since there are three levels of the independent variable, I would use an ANOVA on the data that follows.

	No lecture	Lecture after	Lecture before
	0.26	0.40	0.85
	0.29	0.47	0.88
	0.33	0.44	0.70
	0.15	0.37	0.79
	0.28	0.57	0.90
ΣX	1.31	2.25	4.12
ΣX^2	0.362	1.04	3.42
$\overline{X}$	0.26	0.45	0.82

$$SS_{tot} = 4.83 - \frac{7.68^2}{15} = 0.89$$

$$SS_{treat} = \frac{1.31^2}{5} + \frac{2.25^2}{5} + \frac{4.12^2}{5} - \frac{7.68^2}{15} = 0.82$$

$$SS_{error} = [0.362 - \frac{1.31^2}{5}] + [1.04 - \frac{2.25^2}{5}] + [3.42 - \frac{4.12^2}{5}] = 0.07$$

CHECK: 0.82+0.07=0.89

Source	SS	df	MS	F
Course type	0.82	2	0.41	68.33
Error	0.07	12	0.006	
Total	.082	14		

$F_{.01}$ (2,14 df) = 6.51. The three classroom conditions produced significantly different amounts of test performance. Three Tukey HSD tests produce

HSD (No lecture vs. lecture before) = 16.17

HSD (No lecture vs. lecture after) = 5.48

HSD (Lecture before vs. lecture after) = 10.68

$HSD_{.01}$ = 4.60. There is a significant difference between students who read after they have been lectured to remember more than the other groups. In fact, all the groups showed significant differences. The main point of interest is that students who only attend lecture and who don't read, don't score well!

Chapter 11

Multiple-Choice Questions _____

1. 1   3. 1   5. 1   7. 2   9. 1
11. 4   13. 4   15. 3   17. 4   19. 1

Interpretation _____

1. X   AB Interaction: NS
        A Main Effect: NS
        B Main Effect: Probably significant

    Y   AB Interaction: Probably significant
        A Main Effect: Probably significant
        B Main Effect: NS

3. W AB Interaction: NS
       A Main Effect: Probably significant
       B Main Effect: Probably significant

    X AB Interaction: Probably significant
       A Main Effect: NS
       B Main Effect: Probably significant

    Y AB Interaction: NS
       A Main Effect: Probably significant
       B Main Effect: NS

    Z AB Interaction: NS
       A Main Effect: Probably significant
       B Main Effect: Probably significant

5. All effects are significant beyond the .01 level.

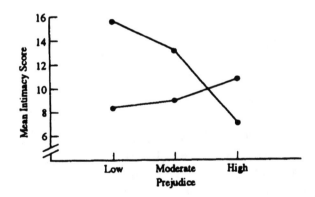

The graph of the cell means indicates that Rokeach is correct for those with low
or moderate prejudice, i.e., prejudice is aroused more by perceived differences in
values than by race. For high-prejudiced people, however, the reverse is true.
Racial differences arouse more prejudice than do differences in values.

Problems _____

1. $SS_{tot} = 6299 - \dfrac{363^2}{24} = 6299 - 5490.3750$
    $= 808.6250$

$SS_{cells} = \dfrac{62^2}{6} + \dfrac{123^2}{6} + \dfrac{114^2}{6} + \dfrac{62^2}{6} - \dfrac{363^2}{24}$

$= 682.667 + 2521.50 + 2166 + 640.667 - 5490.3750$
$= 520.4584$

$SS_{education} = \dfrac{178^2}{12} + \dfrac{185^2}{12} - \dfrac{363^2}{24}$
$= 2640.333 + 2852.0833 - 5490.3750$
$= 2.0416$

$SS_{arguments} = \dfrac{187^2}{12} + \dfrac{176^2}{12} - \dfrac{363^2}{24}$
$= 2914.0833 + 2581.333 - 5490.3750$
$= 5.0146$

$SS_{AB} = 6[(10.667-14.8333-15.5833+15.1250)^2$
$\quad +(20.50-15.4167-15.5833+15.1250)^2$
$\quad +(19.00-14.8333-14.6667+15.1250)^2$
$\quad +(10.3333-15.4167-14.6667+15.1250)^2]$
$\quad = 6[(-4.6249)^2+(4.6250)^2+(4.6250)^2-(-4.6251)^2]$
$\quad = 6(21.3810+21.3906+21.3906+21.3916)=513.3228$

CHECK
$\quad SS_{AB} = 520.4584-2.0416-5.0416$
$\qquad = 513.3752$ (without rounding error)

$$SS_{error} = \left(808 - \frac{64^2}{6}\right) + \left(2603 - \frac{123^2}{6}\right) + \left(2218 - \frac{114^2}{6}\right) + \left(670 - \frac{62^2}{6}\right)$$

$$= 125.333 + 81.50 + 52.00 + 29.33$$
$$= 288.1667$$

CHECK
$$SS_{tot} = 808.6250 = 520.4584 + 288.1667$$

Source	df	SS	MS	F	p
Education(A)	1	2.0416	2.0416	<1.00	>.05
Arguments (B)	1	5.0416	5.0416	<.01	>.05
AB	1	513.3228	513.3228	35.63	<.01
Error	20	288.1667	14.4083		
Total	23	808.6250			

Neither main effect was significant, which, by themselves, would indicate that neither educational level nor type of argument influenced attitude change. The significant interaction effect, however, tells a different story as can be seen from the interaction graph that follows.

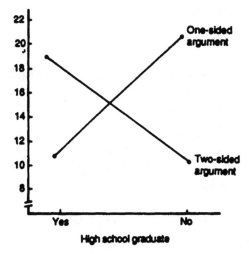

Clearly, both variables influenced attitude change, but the effect of each variable was dependent upon the other. The one-sided argument was effective only for nongraduates, whereas the two-sided argument was effective only for graduates of high school.

Chapter 12

Multiple-Choice Questions _____

1. 1   3. 3   5. 2   7. 4   9. 3
11. 4   13. 3   15. 2   17. 3   19. 1

Short-answer questions _____

1. In a repeated measures design, fewer participants need to be run, there is lower error due to differences between participants, and repeated measures experiments have more statistical power. Two disadvantages are that not all studies can be done as repeated measures, and there is the possibility of carryover effects.

Problems _____

1. $SS_{tot} = 47,623 - \dfrac{725^2}{15} = 47,623 - 35,041.667 = 12,581.333$

$SS_{depth} = \dfrac{75^2}{5} + \dfrac{250^2}{5} + \dfrac{400^2}{5} - \dfrac{725^2}{15} = 1125 + 12,500 + 32,000 -$
$35,041.667 = 45,625 - 35,041.667 = 10,583.333$

$SS_{subjects} = \dfrac{135^2}{3} + \dfrac{170^2}{3} + \dfrac{145^2}{3} + \dfrac{123^2}{3} + \dfrac{152^2}{3} - \dfrac{725^2}{15} =$
$35,461 - 35,041.667 = 419.333$

$SS_{error} = 12,581.333 - 10,583.333 - 419.333 = 1578.667$

Source	SS	df	MS	F	p
Depth	10,583.333	2	5291.667	26.82	< .01
Subjects	419.333	4			
Error	1578.667	8	197.333		
Total	12,581.333	14			

$F_{.01}(2, 8\ df) = 8.65$

$$s_{\bar{x}} = \sqrt{\frac{197.33}{5}} = 6.282 \qquad HSD_{.05} = 4.04 \qquad HSD_{.01} = 5.64$$

HSD (Shallow vs. Medium) = 5.57; $p < .05$

HSD (Shallow vs. Deep) = 10.35; $p < .01$

HSD (Medium vs. Deep) = 4.78; $p < .05$

Interpretation. Memory depends on the level of processing while learning. When processing was deep, participants remembered more than when processing was medium ($p < .05$) and more than when processing was shallow ($p < .01$). In addition, medium processing produced better memory than shallow processing ($p < .05$).

3. $$SS_{tot} = 4436176 - \frac{8134^2}{15} = 25378.93$$

$$SS_{location} = \frac{2676^2}{5} + \frac{2755^2}{5} + \frac{2703^2}{5} - \frac{8134^2}{15} =$$
$$= 4411442 - 4410797.07 = 644.93$$

$$SS_{subjects} = \frac{1547^2}{3} + \frac{1556^2}{3} + \frac{1828^2}{3} + \frac{1524^2}{3} + \frac{1679^2}{3} - \frac{8134^2}{15} =$$
$$4432515.32 - 4410797.07 = 21718.25$$

$$SS_{error} = 25378.93 - 21718.25 - 644.93 = 3015.75$$

Source	SS	df	MS	F	p
location	644.93	2	322.465	0.86	>.05
Subjects	21718.25	4			
Error	3015.75	8	376.97		
Total	512.00	14			

$F_{.05}(2, 8\ df) = 4.46$

Interpretation. There does not appear to be any significant differences between the three conditions. The F value is close to 1 indicating that there is no difference among the means. This is probably due to the small effect caused by the manipulation in the experiment.

Chapter 13

Multiple-Choice Questions _____

1. 3   3. 1   5. 1   7. 2   9. 1
11. 2   13. 2   15. 4   17. 3   19. 2

Interpretation _____

1. Because $\chi^2_{.001}$ (1 df) = 10.83, the null hypothesis can be rejected; the two variables are not independent. In addition, $\phi = 0.40$.

    The conclusion is that those with greater than 5 years of experience tend to be lumpers, and those with less than 5 years of experience tend to be splitters. There is a medium to large effect of experience on anthropologist's view of how the world is put together.

Problems _____

1. $\chi^2 = \dfrac{32[(10)(12) - (8)(2)]^2}{(18)(14)(12)(20)} = 5.72$ $\phi = \sqrt{\dfrac{5.72}{32}} = 0.42$

$\chi^2_{.05}$ (1 *df*) = 3.84. Therefore, reject the null hypothesis and conclude that living conditions make a difference in survival rates. Those that were isolated were more likely to be alive than those that lived together. The effect of the living conditions on survival was intermediate between a medium effect and a large effect.

3. Goodness-of-fit.

	O	E	$O - E$	$\dfrac{(O-E)^2}{E}$
brown	222	226.8	-4.8	0.102
yellow	149	151.2	-2.2	0.032
Red	132	151.2	-19.2	2.438
Blue	102	75.6	26.4	9.219
green	44	75.6	-31.6	13.208
orange	107	75.6	31.4	13.042
Σ	756	756		$\chi^2 = 38.041$

$\chi^2_{.001}$ (5 *df*) = 20.52. The null hypothesis is rejected, $p < .001$. The distribution of colors in my bag was significantly different from the distribution advertised by the Mars company. In particular, there were too many blue and orange candies and not enough green candies.

5. This is a goodness-of-fit test of a 50:50 hypothesis. The expected value for each gender is 1,940,447, which is the total number of births divided by 2. Arranging calculations into a table,

	O	E	$O - E$	$\dfrac{(O-E)^2}{E}$
boys	1,985,596	1,940,447	45,149	1050.5
Girls	1,895,298	1,940,447	-45,149	1050.5
Σ	3,880,894	3,880,894		$\chi^2 = 2101.0$

$\chi^2_{.001}$ $(1df)$ = 10.83. Reject the hypothesis that girls and boys are born in equal numbers. Boys are born in greater numbers than girls. Indeed, the results for this one year mirror the results of many years in many countries: the birth rate is about 105 males for every 100 females (but the infant survival rate for males is lower).

Chapter 14

Multiple-Choice Questions _____

1. 3   3. 2   5. 1   7. 2   9. 2
11. 5(6.5) 13. 4   15. 2 17. 4

Interpretation _____

1. A. Mann-Whitney U test
    B. Spearman r_s
    C. Wilcoxon matched-pairs signed-ranks T test

3. With N = 9, a T value of 5.0 or less is required for significance at α = .05. Because the obtained T is 5.5, the hypothesis that the difference between the before and after scores is due to chance cannot be rejected.

5. A Wilcoxon-Wilcox multiple-comparisons test is appropriate.

	0 (73)	20 (54)	40 (44.5)	60 (27.5)
20(54)	19			
40(44.5)	28.5	9.5		
60(27.5)	45.5	26.5	17	
80(11)	62**	43	33.5	16.5

* $p < .05$
** $p < .01$

The conclusion from these data (and from Gates and many others) is that self-recitation improves recall. The trend in the data is steadily upward; the more self-recitation, the better the recall.

Problems _____

1.

Time on Target (T.O.T) in Seconds	Pilot Competency Score	T.O.T. Rank	Pilot Score Rank	D	D^2
18	37	4	7	3	9
15	57	6	2	4	16
28	63	1	1	0	0
25	41	2	6	4	16
9	31	8	8	0	0
17	51	5	3	2	4
23	42	3	5	2	4
11	45	7	4	3	9
					$\Sigma=58$

$$rs = 1 - \frac{6\left(\sum D^2\right)}{N(N^2-1)} = 1 - \frac{6(58)}{8(63)} = .31$$

3.

Frontal	Rank
54	14
31	8
18	3
26	6
39	10
42	11
45	12
Σ	64

Parietal	Rank
47	13
30	7
12	1
17	2
21	4
25	5
35	9
Σ	41

CHECK: $64+41=105=\dfrac{(14)(15)}{2}$

$$U_{frontal} = (7)(7) + \frac{(7)(8)}{2} - 64 = 13$$

$$U_{parietal} = (7)(7) + \frac{(7)(8)}{2} - 41 = 36$$

From Table H, $U_{.05}=8$

There is no significant difference in the number of errors made by rats that lost 40 percent of their frontal lobe and rats that lost 40 percent of their parietal lobes.

5. I would use the Mann-Whitney U test.

Group 1	Group 2
1	2
3	6
4	7
5	8
9	10
$\Sigma=22$	$\Sigma=33$

CHECK: $22+33=55=\dfrac{(10)(11)}{2}$

$$U_{Group1} = (5)(5) + \frac{(5)(6)}{2} - 22 = 18$$

$$U_{Group2} = (5)(5) + \frac{(5)(6)}{2} - 33 = 7$$

From Table H, $U_{.05}=1$

There is no significant difference on ranked IQ scores in this study.

Chapter 15 Answers

1. Chi Square test for independence

2. Independent samples t test

3. One-way ANOVA

4. Spearman r

5. Chi Square test for independence

6. Mann-Whitney U test

7. One sample t test

8. Regression equation

9. One-factor, repeated measures ANOVA

10. One-way ANOVA

11. Correlation coefficient

12. Mann-Whitney U test

13. Factorial ANOVA

14. Independent-sample t test

15. Effect size estimate

16. Wilcoxon matched-pairs, signed-ranks T test

17. Paired-samples t test

18. Regression equation

19. Independent-samples *t* test

20. Factorial ANOVA

Appendix A – Arithmetic and Algebra Review

Problems _____

1. 15.844

3. 34.657

5. 373.817

7. 65.28

9. 10.64

11. 0.026

13. 5.246

15. 18.25

17. .50 + .05 +.125 = .875

19. .8571 + .625 + .9048 = 2.387

21. .375 - .2 = .175

23. .2 - .125 = .075

25. .6667 x .5714 = .381

27. .7 x .5 x .6667 = .233

29. $.5 \div .3333 = 1.500$

31. $.6316 \div .8571 = .737$

33. 1

35. −55

37. −3

39. −2

41. 10

43. 140

45. 2

47. −2.167

49. $\dfrac{15}{27} = .556$

51. $.22 \times 27 = 5.94$ or 6

53. 11

55. 2

57. −8, 28

59. −11.25, -4.75

61. 36

63. 342.25

Complex Problems _____

65. $\dfrac{19}{3} = 6.3333$

67. $\dfrac{(66-12.5)+(75-12.8)}{9} = \dfrac{51.6+62.2}{9} = \dfrac{113.8}{9} = 12.644$

69. $\dfrac{25-72}{53.55} = \dfrac{-47}{53.55} = -.878$

71. $\dfrac{-6.8}{\sqrt{\dfrac{73}{9}(.1667+.3333)}} = \dfrac{-6.8}{\sqrt{(8.111)(.5)}} = \dfrac{-6.8}{\sqrt{4.0556}} = \dfrac{-6.8}{2.0138} = -3.3767$

73. $\sqrt{\dfrac{(68-12.5)(54-24.2)}{42}} = \sqrt{\dfrac{55.5+29.8}{42}} = \sqrt{\dfrac{85.3}{42}} = \sqrt{2.031} = 1.425$

75. $x + 5 = (3)(4.25)$
$x = 12.75 - 5$
$x = 7.75$

77. $\dfrac{8}{4} = 2x - 2$
$2 + 2 = 2x$
$4 = 2x$
$2 = x$

APPENDIX B – Grouped Frequency Distributions and Central Tendency

Problems _____

1. These data could be grouped with $i = 3$ or $i = 5$. We used $i = 5$ with multiples of 5 at the midpoints. Class intervals and central tendency statistics for $i = 3$ are given at the end of this answer.

Class Interval	f	fX
123-127	1	125
118-122	2	240
113-117	2	230
108-112	2	220
103-107	4	420
98-102	7	700
93-97	4	380
88-92	4	360
83-87	1	85
78-82	3	240
73-77	1	75
Σ	31	3075

$$\bar{X} = \frac{3075}{31} = 99.19$$

Median location $= \dfrac{N+1}{2} = \dfrac{31+1}{2} = 16$. Counting from the bottom of the distribution, the are 13 IQ's below 98-102 so the median is located among the 7 IQ's in that interval. The Median IQ is the midpoint of the interval, 100.

The mode is the midpoint of the interval 98-102 because that interval has more frequencies than the others: modal IQ = 100.

A mean IQ of 99.2 indicates that damage to the left cerebrum of women does not impair their IQ scores. With $i = 3$, the lowest interval is 72-74; $\bar{X} = 98.55$, Median = 101; Mode = 100.

3A.

N = 32
Median = 49

Class Interval	X	f
66-68	67	1
63-65	64	0
60-62	61	3
57-59	58	4
54-56	55	1
51-53	52	3
48-50	49	5
45-47	46	0
42-44	45	6
39-41	40	5
36-38	37	2
33-35	34	1
30-32	31	1

3B.

$N = 35$
Median = 30

Class Interval	X	f
68-72	70	1
63-67	65	0
58-62	60	2
53-57	55	0
48-52	50	4
43-47	45	2
38-42	40	5
33-37	35	1
28-32	30	3
23-27	25	2
18-22	20	4

13-17	15	5
8-12	10	2
3-7	5	2
-2-2	0	2

References

Berk, L.E. (2000). *Child Development* (5th ed.). Boston: Allyn & Bacon.

Breland, H.M. (1974). Birth order, family configuration, and verbal achievement. *Child Development, 45,* 1011-1019.

Cohen, I. B. (March, 1984). Florence Nightengale. *Scientific American, 250,* 128-137.

Cohen, J. (1992). Statistical Power analysis. *Current Directions in Psychological Science, 1,* 98-101.

Craik, F.I.M., & Tulving, E. (1975). Depth of processing and retention of words in episodic memory. *Journal of Experimental Psychology: General, 104,* 268-294.

D'Agostino, R.B. (1973). How much does a 40-pound box of bananas weight? In F. Mosteller et al., *Statistics by example: Detecting patterns.* Reading, MA: Addison-Wesley.

Gates, A.I. (1917). Recitation as a factor in memorizing. *New York Archives of Psychology,* No. 40.

Hovland, C., Lumsdaine, A., & Sheffield, F. (1949). *Experiments on mass communication.* Princeton, NJ: Princeton University Press.

Hulse, S.H. (1973). Patterned reinforcement. In G.H. Bower (Ed.), *The psychology of learning and motivation,* Vol. 7, New York: Academic Press.

Lazarus, R.S., & Alfert, E. (1964). Shortcircuiting of threat by experimentally altering cognitive and social appraisal. *Journal of Abnormal and Social Psychology, 69,* 195-205.

Luchins, A.S. (1942). Mechanization in problem solving: The effect of *einstellung*. *Psychology Monographs, 54,* No. 6.

Matsumoto, D., Kasri, F., & Kooken, K. (1999). American-Japanese cultural differences in judgements of expression intensity and subjective experience. *Cognition and Emotion, 13,* 201-218.

Milgram, S. (1963). Behavioral study of obedience. *Journal of Abnormal and Social Psychology, 67,* 371-378.

Miller, N.E., & Bugelski, R. (1948). Minor studies in aggression II: The influence of frustrations imposed by the in-group on attitudes expressed toward out-groups. *Journal of Psychology, 25,* 437-442.

Murphy, K.R., & Davidshofer, C.O. (1991). *Psychological testing: Principles and applications* (2nd ed.). Englwood Cliffs, NJ: Prentice Hall.

O'Brien, E. J., Albrecht, J. E., Hakala, C. M., & Rizzella, M. L. (1995). Activation and suppression of antecedents during reinstatement. *Journal of Experimental Psychology: Learning, Memory and Cognition, 21,* 626-634.

Ree, M.J., & Earles, J.A. (1992). Intelligence is the best predictor of job performance. *Current Directions in Psychological Science, 1,* 86-89.

Sokol, M.M (1982). James McKeen Cattell and the failure of anthropometric mental testing, 1890-1901. In W.R. Woodward and M.G. Ash (Eds.). *The problematic science: Psychology in nineteenth-century thought.* New York: Praeger.

Spatz, C., & Jones, S.D. (1971). Starvation anorexia as an explanation of "self-starvation" of rats living in activity wheels. *Journal of Comparative and Physiological Psychology, 77,* 313-317.

Spatz, T.S. (1991). Improving breast self-examination training by using the 4MAT instructional model. *Journal of Cancer Education, 6,* 179-183.

Statistical abstract of the United States: 2001 (122 ed.) (2001). Washington, D.C.:U.S. Bureau of the Census.

Stodtbeck, F. (1951). Husband-wife interactions over revealed differences. *American Sociological Review, 16* 468-473.

Turnbull, C.M. (1961). *The forest people.* New York: Simon and Schuster.

Van Cott, H.P., & Kinkade, R.G., (Eds.) (1972). *Human engineering guide to equipment design* (Rev. ed.). Joint Army-Navy-Air Force Steering Committee, Washington, D.C.: U.S. Government Printing Office.

Warden, C.J. (1931). *Animal motivation studies: The albino rat.* New York: Columbia University Press.

Wender, P.H., & Klein, D.F. (1981). The promise of biological psychiatry. *Psychology Today, 15(2),* 25-41.

Zajonc, R.B., & Bargh, J. (1980). Birth order, family size, and decline of SAT scores. *American Psychologist, 35,* 662-668.